NEW GENERATION BEATS
2025 ANTHOLOGY

NATIONAL BEAT POETRY FOUNDATION, INC.

Published by
New Generation Beat Publications

ISBN: 978-1-957654-22-5

Debbie Tosun Kilday - Editing & Cover Design.

Human Error Publishing - Editing & Formatting

The 2025 New Generation Beats Anthology

The National Beat Poetry Foundation's mission is to continue the legacy of the original beat generation, but to evolve into the future with a new generation of beat writers, not afraid to write about things that matter and to not be silenced. The goal is to be inclusive not exclusive, and to provide a safe and respectful atmosphere where poets can share.

TABLE OF CONTENTS

Su Zi

legacy

whom shall i haunt
will this alto still weave your ear
my visage a flicker
what incantations shall become your tattoos
have you felt me
nearby
my famous scent will yield to other bodies
(the horses know this, as do all them all who know my color)
have you felt me
next to next
my noble bones and your
in ancestral disbelief
because i and i were flesh to you
may this ever be your madness.

Su Zi was honored to be included in the 2024 New Generation Beats Anthology. Recently performed at the 2025 St Augustine Poetry Fest, participating poet with the Sunshine State Festival of the Book, and resident of the beleaguered Ocala National Forest.Zoeglossia Fellow Multiple titles in publication, with a forthcoming title accepted by Finish Line Press.

Tracey Zee

Traveling Light

Just off the gravel road
to my mother's house
twilight illuminates little bluestem grass
A small white house
sits on the horizon
In the sea of golden possibility.
Eyes of black angus cows
line the fence
Their blank stares
darkening with kindness.
I let the car idle
And think of home
As they nibble tiny tendrils
Between the barbed wire.
Whatever it was I lost, whatever I wept for
was once
a wild and gentle thing
Like the small, dark eyes
loving me in secret.
I lean back
and watch the brilliant hues fade
into distant memories.
Never return
to the places
you try so hard to forget.

Tracey Zee is a poet and public servant living in Austin, TX, where she has worked tirelessly to help the unhoused people in her community find stable and supportive housing. She also works as the publishingassistant for Hercules Publishing, a small indie publishing company based out of Albuquerque, NM. Her poetry orbits the poignant and banal moments of everyday life. She recently traveled with Vagaband Poetry Caravan Tour, spreading the message of hope and unity, and performing her poetry in front of audiences for the firs time.

Zohreh Zadbood

A Warm Hug

If only I can draw my left hand over, yearning
solace on my right side
my right hand glides, weaving
a silent bond to my left
I will ignite the light
inner me.
its wick burns
embers trail down the spine
each touch, a new sting of fire.
striving to hush them
I wonder in a daze
blind to their essence
I hold onto my true self.

Zohreh Zadbood is an aspiring Iranian storyteller, photographer and poet writing in both English and Persian. A recent NYU graduate, she is completing her MFA in Creative Writing at The New School. Her work has appeared in The Coalition, The Kenyon Review, and The Los Angeles Press, among other places.

Hiromi Yoshida

Sequel to Allen Ginsberg's "America"

America, why are your guns pointed in every wrong
direction?
America, why are your coffers filled with tears and blood
and bullets?
America, why are you keeping a million dead sunflowers
in your unkempt backyards?
America, why are your taxpayers calling the President
the n-word when they have better
things to do like report to work at 8:00 AM EDT?
(I'm talking to you with a mouthful of exorbitant teeth.)
America, how can we learn to pray in the sanctified
churches of imagination and call it
neither neurosis nor masturbation?
America, how can we petition our senators without
libeling them needlessly?
America, when are you going to tighten your belt
appropriately to eliminate the problem of obesity?
America, when will you admit that you've had enough Jello?
America, when will your libraries and schools and
churches become sufficiently bulletproof?
America, when will you quit telling the homeless to gohome?
America, when will the dust of your roads settle in all the
right places?
America, when will your dumpsters quit overflowing with
wholesale yard sale
commodities?
America, when will you quit blaming your victims?
(Will you gallop away on your high horse again?)
America, when will you stop blaming all your problems on
immigrants, liberals, and
Daylight Savings?
America, when will you quit feeding your people rib-eyed
steak and chocolate mint ice
cream?
America, when will your people quit taking a dump in
their neighbors 'backyards?
America, when will they learn to clean up after

themselves without the help of Mr.
Clean?
America, when will they learn that Timothy McVeigh information was actually "TMI"?
America, when will you quit shooting heroin up your rainbow-colored arms?
America, when will you embrace your rainbow-colored people?
America, when will your acolytes learn to masturbate properly?
America, when will your avocados ripen at the right time?
America, when will your children know it's time to go home?
America, when will the peep-show of government transparency come to an end?
America, when will death cease to be the exorbitant price for being gay?
America, when will we hear the Zen thunderclap of one arthritic hand?
America, when will your politicians quit splitting pubic hairs in the chambers of
commerce and masturbation?
America, when will your wet dreams evaporate into desiccated bone reality?
America, when will Allen Ginsberg's ghost appear before us in the lonely hopeless wild
glare of imagination—in the tattered regalia of madness and dystopia—like a
discarded homosexual angel?
America, it's time for us all to pay up with all the green pennies we've gathered from the
sidewalk cracks on our makeshift Wall Streets.

Hiromi Yoshida, an author of two full-length poetry collections and five poetry chapbooks, is a finalist for the New Women's Voices Poetry Prize, and a semifinalist for the Gerald Cable Book Award. She is the Poetry Editor of Flying Island Journal, and serves on the board of directors for the Writers Guild at Bloomington, while coordinating the Guild's Last Sunday Poetry reading series. She is collaborating with Jim Canary at the Lilly Library to curate a pop-up exhibition for the Guild's Allen Ginsberg at 100 celebration in April 2026.

Eric Allen Yankee

God Bomb

Don't know what the fuck they're doing as they prod bomb,
Just another day in the cracked world, my broken God bomb.

It may be another day before the fire burns itself out,
another day of lies to tell and corpses to applaud bomb.

Many see an explosion as a bright thing in these times,
spreading metal to the wind and making an awed bomb.

Men race to their deaths in all times, seek eternal love
in the metallic face and bright orange light in a clawed bomb.

There is no end, no ceasefire, no place to ever belong now,
only a hole in the ground where children once stood, flawed bomb.

And I am just another protest poet, lost in the cave of life,
only to find that someday I too may meet a big fraud bomb.

Eric Allen Yankee is a member of the League of Revolutionaries for a New America. His work has appeared in many places online and in print, including anthologies by Vagabond Books, the Revolutionary Poet's Brigade, and more. He is the author of five poetry chapbooks.

Lorna Wood

Self-Fulfilling Dreams

When we were multitudes crying out for him,

The Maganificent Pumpkin came to us in a dream,

embraced us with his pumpkin arms—

No questions, please.

They're rude, and anyway,

we won't wake up.

He forgave us our trespassing

and told us we could skip

forgiving, for only we, his belov.d,

would occupy this patch

(because we made him)

world without end—

                                        or at least

until we trampled the vines

and fouled the water

and covered the ground

with refuse and excrement.

He has grown gross and swollen

on our adoration.

His stench is over the land.

But still we do not wake up

because in our nightmares

each of us is only a child

with a blanket

in an empty world.

Lorna Wood is a teacher, musician, and writer in Chicago. A featured writer in the erbacce-prize contest, she has a Ph.D in English from Yale and international publications. Her poem, "I Always Knew It Would Be This Way, I just didn't expect it to be so soon," appeared in the New Generation Beats 2022 anthology, and her debut collection, The Great Garbage Patch (Alien Buddha Press) appeared in 2023. She has also published fiction, creative nonfiction, and scholarly essays.

Linda Bratcher Wlodyka

The Beat of our Lives

We take in the sites, hear the sounds

smell aromas that infiltrate our brain

retrieve selected memories. Foliage, water,

soil, stone, mountains and how much sky

is visible between branches of a tree's canopy

reveal what has transpired before birth.

Yet the earth's tilt--could it become askew

over years of rotation? Can our senses become

heightened, our awareness realized, as experiences

change along with perspective? Yes I believe this is so.

We age, live a life well-lived

or as best we can under human conditions

& unforeseen complexities. We succumb to

our own tilt of perspective. Embrace the silver moon,

bluing sky, puffed-up clouds, translucent raindrops,

gather them in a basket, a hat, or within your cupped
hands.

Praise what is now! Celebrate blessings. Shout, sing,
chant, dance!

Never be silenced! Your word is your strength.

It carves your path, it begs you follow through.

Do the words keeps us alive?

At its core words are: the beat of our lives.

Yes! Your cup is not half anything,

You already filled it to the brim!

Linda Bratcher Wlodyka is the Massachusetts Beat Poet Laureate from 2023-2025, is a retired educator, an avid lover of fantasy, whimsy and mystical places. She has published 3 chapbooks and one full-length collection, If Brambles were Bookends, (Human Error Publishing 2023). Her best advice to anyone is: “Do what you enjoy and do not wait another moment to begin. Appreciate everything and anyone who influences that joy.”

Francine Witte

Blues Man

sax man
cat man
playin 'for me
as I wait
for my train.

Blues man
sax man
cat man
you know
I been
scratched
and I
went back
again,

and your
hand-paws
are findin'
the saddest
refrain.

Blues man
sax man
cat man
you are startin'
the sweetest
parade
in my brain.

Blues man
sax man
cat man
you are
the only
good reason
for pain.

Francine Witte's newest poetry book, Some Distant Pin of Light, has just been published by Cervena Barva Press. She is a recent recipient of a Pushcart Prize. She lives in New York City.

Matthew Wilks

A Conversation With Myself

You're ugly.
You're worthless.
You don't have a purpose.

You can't do anything right.
Don't try to fight.
Enough of this plight.
You know I'm right!
You are nothing without me.
You will never be free.

Wait a minute
Wait a minute!
and you will see
I am BECOMING me.
This is my lightest
I am shining the brightest
I have ever been.
I am going to win.
Someday you won't have this much power
And I will tower over you and this prescription of
selfcrucifixion.

Think so, do you?
It's like I knew you.
We have been here so many times before.
My God this is such a chore!
We do this dance almost daily
This has gotten so crazy!
You will never leave me.
I think it's time you believe me!
Just admit that you love me
Don't try to shove me away.
So surrender to my say
Come on, let's play.

No.
No!

I refuse.
Today you lose.
Take a look at this fitness
It's time that you witness
the truth.

I don't need you anymore.
It's time we settle the score.
All you ever did was hurt me.
True you never desert me
But now I'm gonna assert me.

Go away and leave me alone.
Yes!
This is me.
Hello you! I've grown.
You should have known this day was coming
I am shoving
Past you and the hurt because I've learnt I was always
Enough.
No this is not fluff.
I am just discerning
From the past 12 years of learning
I am better off without you.
No, I don't doubt you
But I am not about you.
My identity is clear
Take the cloth off the mirror.
I am here
I do not fear you.

Matthew Wilks is a writer residing in NE Ohio. He is a graduate of the American Musical and Dramatic Academy in New York City and has been performing, directing and teaching theatre professionally for over 14 years. His written work can be seen in several anthologies from "Poetry is Life Publishing" His work deals almost exclusively with themes of mental health, spreading the message "You are not alone

Ron Whitehead

Jack and Jesus put Beatitude in Beat

For Jack Kerouac, Beat meant "...to be in a state of beatitude, like St. Francis, trying to love all life, trying to be utterly sincere with everyone, practicing endurance, kindness."

Jack and Jesus put Beatitude in Beat.

Kerouac tried his best to cultivate a "joy of heart" in a "mad modern world of multiplicities and millions."

People came from everywhere to hear Jesus speak. It turned into an all day deal. By early afternoon folks were getting hungry but only a few had brought food. Jesus asked his disciples to feed the multitudes. The disciples said, "No way. Impossible."

A kid came wandering by with five loaves of bread and two fish.

Jesus said, "Hey kid, come here." The kid said, "Yes, mister, what is it?" Jesus said, "You want to help me perform a miracle?"

The kid's eyes got big. The kid stared at Jesus to the count of 1, 2, 3 then said, "Sure, I'd like to see that. What do I need to do?" Jesus said, "Give my disciples your bread and your fish and watch what happens."

The kid handed over, watched for a while then launched into helping the disciples as they all fed 5,000 hungry people who had come to hear Jesus speak.

When the kid heard Jesus say, "Blessed are those who mourn, for they will be comforted." he stopped to listen.

Jack Kerouac was of French Canadian descent. He was born and raised, for his first 17 years, in Lowell, Massachusetts. That's when Jack hit the road.

Kerouac was Catholic but for years he sought and found solace in Buddhism.

Like Trappist monk and prolific Kentucky author Thomas Merton, Kerouac never left Catholicism.

Like famous Kentucky author Hunter S. Thompson, Kerouac wasn't able to escape his deepening alcoholism, which finally killed him.

The entire time he struggled and suffered, Kerouac kept

seeking the light, through his words. And through his tears of sorrow, in a strange state of joy, he wrote.
Writing kept Jack Kerouac alive. Writing saved his life.
And his writing saves our lives, as we struggle with the pain, the suffering, the mundanity of living, of life.
Kerouac sought to juxtapose the seemingly irreconcilable differences inherent in what it means to be fully human.
And despite his torment, as a seeker, he became, through his writing, a beatific saint.
Jesus was crucified. Kerouac drank himself to death.
Holy Jesus. Saint Kerouac.
Jack and Jesus put Beatitude in Beat.
Jack and Jesus become perfect after life.
They laugh and in tenor sing old folk songs and broke down blues.
They are ageless.
Their new home is a flower garden.
They smell of roses and Night-blooming cereus.
They are finished with sadness.
They are sun and bone bright.
Happiness grows on them.

Photo by Jinn Bug.

Ron Whitehead, U.S. National Lifetime Beat Poet Laureate

Lynn White

Tired of Waiting

From Langston Hughes to Ray Davies,
from the political to the personal
and back again,
back and forth,
back and forth.
From Kissinger to the newbie
pretenders standing in line
moving back and forth,
back and forth.
From Stockholm to The Hague
back and forth,
back and forth.
We are so tired,
so very tired,
but all we can do is wait
to see where we shall find them.

Lynn White lives in north Wales. Her work is influenced by issues of social justice and events, places and people she has known or imagined. She is especially interested in exploring the boundaries of dream, fantasy and reality. She was shortlisted in the Theatre Cloud 'War Poetry for Today' competition and has been nominated for Pushcarts, Best of the Net and a Rhysling Award. Find Lynn at: https://lynnwhitepoetry.blogspot.com and https://www.facebook.com/Lynn-White Poetry-1603675983213077/

Jeff Weddle

Consider This

Do we grieve now
for the little lost souls,
or do we fear them?
They are hungry
and we might give them bread
or they might take our blood.
Do we hear them singing
or is that our own wail?
Arm yourself with something.
Love is best,
and charity.
You will need a mighty shield
and a true map of the heart.
Get moving. There are many choices,
but only one path takes you home.

Jeff Weddle teaches in the School of Library and Information Studies at the University of Alabama. He is the Alabama Beat Poet Laureate (2024-2026).

Karen Warinsky

Album Cover

It hit me hard there in my little dorm room as the words started

J i G L I n G

on the page and I called Barry to tell him it had kicked in and Irene from down the hall (who always let us watch MASH in her room on Tuesday nights) thought it would be funny to put **a dust mop** in my face because she knew we'd dropped acid, and the smell made me ***panic.*** I rubbed my hands together for comfort and they turned into **big fleshy globs** and my last coherent thought for a while was

"That's not good."

The six of us walked outside all together in the January crisp holding hands like children behind their teacher, letting Barry lead us (he'd tripped so often) but I only remember bits of thosefirst hours; colors, sounds, no real comprehension of where I was, orthat I was.Coming back inside we trudged up the stairwell together

and Sue gave me something to drink,

became the cement steps

and my legs

and we all split up at some point
and Sue took me over to her new guy friend's room on the 6th floor and he seemed *kinder* and **smarter** than her guy friends on the 4th floor and I did feel bad the next day after I realized I picked up one of his album covers and tore it in two saying:

"Nothing matters anymore!"

And that's when he began talking to me in a very personal way till I returned to myself me what

ask was

don't on

but turntable that

and don't ask me his name.

Karen Warinsky has published poetry widely since 2011. She is the author of four collections: Gold in Autumn (2020) andSunrise Ruby (2022 Human Error Publishing,) Dining with War(2023 Alien Buddha Press) and Beauty & Ashes (Kelsay Books, 2025). Her poem "Mirage" won first place in the 2024 Ekphrastic Poetry Trust, she is a 2023 Best of the Net nominee and a former finalist of the Montreal International Poetry Contest. Warinsky coordinates Poets at Large, a group that performs spoken word in MA and CT. https://karenwarinskypoetry.wordpress.com.

George Wallace

How Jack Said Goodbye

It was the end of the road
it was the end of the line
it was the end of the kicks
he could wear it with pride
he could wear it with abandon,
like a good plaid shirt on a cool autumn day
he could wear it like jazz
he could wing it like the Buddha
he could laugh dream dream cry
outrace hotrods, out talk Proust
he could sing a song that went around and around in his
head all day, like Mel Torme

But the sad and the tragic and the mad kept coming
the sad and the tragic, the suffering and the mad
down the endless highway inside his head
and in the end, he never said goodbye
just his slippers propped up on the table,
his back against the wall, and the sad mysterious
inevitability of it all,

He never looked up to say goodbye.

George Wallace (b.1949 NY, USA), Writer in residence,Walt Whitman Birthplace. Author of 42 chapbooks and 5 spoken word albums in US, UK,Italy, Greece, Macedonia, Portugal, Saudi Arabia, India, Spain. Major international poetry festival prizes and appearances, inc. Orpheus Prize (BG); Alexander Prize, Aristotle Medal (GR); Silk Road Prize, Poet of the Year (CN); Naim Frasheri Laureateship (MK); Corona d'Oro (AL); Naji Naaman Literary Prize (LB), Medellin (CO, Ledbury (GB), Lyric Recovery/Carnegie Hall (US). National Beat Poet Laureate/Lifetime Next Generation Beat Poet (US); Honorary Doctorate, CiESART/Royal Academy 2024 (SP).

Benito Vila

Dazzling Diamond Sparkle Soul Floating in the Sky

Dazzling diamond sparkle soul floating in the sky.
I see it in your eyes, you've discovered you're in a dream,
flash, the red-hat freedom warriors act like
they're the ones fighting for their life,
rebel flags on their pickups, so proud of their guns,
without the discipline and empathy of real soldiers,
all they want to do is point and shoot, post images,
pain makers, nothing more, desperate to please daddy.

It is finished, he cried, breathless. Jesus knew for sure
that nothing at all happens in the outside world, that
what happens takes place within, beyond the reach of
men and god and law, and that was his crime, to insist
the kingdom of heaven was within, aglow, present,
eternal, a wisdom we each have always, awake, aware
that it cannot be identified by m or f, a full seed ready,
inside us, light given from beyond, a love ready to bloom.

A womb for our wounds, the naked destruction
of my mind, asking "why" when there are so many
other questions to ask, the horses are out of the barn, t
he other team is ninety feet away from winning,
my loved ones are nowhere to be seen,
what can I do now, where do I go for help,
how does my song go, who holds my heaviness,
my resistance, now that I see what I want slip away.

In another world, a wailing mother holds her
faceless child, a child who will never grow old,
an immortal, the child who made her who she was
before the hate came and took everything it could,
while in Moscow, Washington, Jerusalem and Gaza,
con men gamble like they're masters, being nothing
more than murderers, gangsters and thugs, rolling dice,
counting pips, taking lives.

The magician, the fool, the blind man look at life differently,
only knowing right now, like at any time we can disappear
and you may say that doesn't make much sense,
that to live that way makes nothing matter,
like everything can suddenly change, birds bark,
dogs sing, morning comes with a house on fire,
black smoke, money stuffed in a drawer inside,
father wants to go back, but looks at his girls and doesn't.

Either or, either one, anyone got a pill for this?
It's like every modern society suffers from a mental
illness, maybe our whole species is readying itself for
extinction, ignoring what made us so different, so practical,
before we got addicted to mine, to more, to not enough, to
the fear we'll never make it, hooked on feeling lost, being
adrift rather than sailing, a punishment for going out alone,
for forgetting the truth when the time comes to rely on it.

To worry on and on is to strangle your mind, to harness it
with doubt and disbelief, setting fire to the work
that's due tomorrow, a sort of sabotage that feeds our
loves, our courage, our let's do this now, to monsters with
no teeth but plenty of hunger, ready to take you
where you can't see, think or feel, and then,
suddenly, you don't know what's happening next,
dazzling diamond sparkle soul floating in the sky.

Benito Vila lives in a remote fishing village on Mexico's Pacific coast. He writes since he can't draw or collage. Since moving to Mexico in early 2022, his poetry has been published by several literary journals.

Chryssa Velissariou

Only Static

I can no longer write normally.
I can only write horrific pieces—
Leftover lines from yesterday's bombing.
Like a thriller.
As horrific as the crimes I suspect
when I stare at the wall across from me.

We shattered the mirrors ourselves.
Our own grimaces disturbed us too much.
We prefer shadows,
and sealing wax in our ears.
Yet the Man-Eaters make sure
the world knows they commit their crimes openly...

We, the Few,
are mostly surrounded by Man-Eaters.
They don't devour others
out of hunger or pleasure.
They do it to keep leading.
They hand out consent forms,
absolution documents with protocol numbers.

They stockpile the living,
tolerate their screams—
(or is it we who tolerate them?)
their massive, starving eyes,
the deformed outlines of the nearly dead.

Each execution has a designated Slaughterhouse:
- • “Progress.”
- • “Development.”
- • “National Security.”
- • “We respect human life.”
- • “Zero tolerance for lawlessness.”

And we—on the other side—Silence.
Eyes down.
“I wash my hands
of the blood of this innocent man.”

None of us dares to admit
we seek refuge in lethargy
because it spares us
the realization of our complicity.

You see, the chain on our feet

isn’t a “slip-on, slip-off” kind.
The Wretched must work endlessly.
Grateful that we weren’t eaten too.
Grateful to exist—even as invisible.
Grateful for the heating.
And the free rent once a year.
As long as we don’t make noise...

Sometimes, someone starts to scream.
That’s the perfect moment
for those tired of being Beneath
and Threatened
to become the Executioners themselves.

The one who screamed vanishes.

And we, now even more “reasonable” slaves,
don’t even turn to fight.
“Better cowards than slaughtered,” we say...

Still, I often wonder—

what would happen
if we all started screaming at once?
Are we truly the Few?
Or is that just another excuse?

You opened your mouth to answer me—
I froze.
No voice came out.
Only *televised static*.

Chryssa Velissariou is a physicist of wonder, a poet of empathy, and an environmental educator. Director of the Senior High School of Domeniko and founder of Smiling Sketches, she bridges art, science, and sustainability. Her poetry has been honored by the National Beat Poetry Foundation (NBPF), and recognized in the USA, Canada, and global events she curates. She was also awarded by the Greek Ministry of Education. Her work transforms learning into a poetic act of resistance and connection.

Jon Veilleux

Buzz of War

buzz of war
Proclamations The of the need to fight
Using your kids
Not theirs
Using your money
Not theirs
I have no quarrel with the others
I don't even know them
but
I believe they have the same needs and wants as us
They have families they love
They have land they cherish
They want to live in peace
I do know the ones calling for us to kill or be killed
Their shadowy, slippery rhetoric
Their flag waving so called patriotism
Their craven greed
For the spoils of war
And I know
Who is the REAL enemy

Jon Veilleux is a retired hitch-hiker sitting in his suburban home writing bad poetry and hoping to come out of retirement and travel the roads again in search of the lost humanity of America.

Ahmet Ali Uzun

Dua Bohemya

a rhythm plays from afar
in the smoke rising to the sky
/the fog covers the night./

drumbeats in the heart of the **Bozkir** .
—count your lost steps.—

the K.m awakens;
in the eyes of the blaze wrapped
in the fur of the fox
within a "existence" no soul has yet beheld.

an owl as old as the wind wings into the night
and as newborn as the sun
the sound of the trees bends to the earth,
the exhaustion sparks in the breath of the horses

drawn in his hands,
the stars, the galaxies, and the universe
the moment was the memory, of the water
running down
his palms.

the breath of the **Bozkir** .
the sound of the taut strings
belonging to a far, drunk, fierce sage
carrying a nomadic past on his back
          he tells,
the water listens,
          dances,
the fire burns,
          screams,
the night keeps silence.

listen to him, eyes closed, beyond the boundaries
for everything has a soul
Anadolu is an ancient prayer

still echoing in the sky.

Ahmet Ali Uzun
(b. 2002, Bursa) studies Geological Eng. at Istanbul Tech. University. In ITU, he was the editor of ArıYorumfanzine, have revived the Literature Club and is the chief of .. Virgül. He has 3 poetry books: Mitologya, Alabildiğine Karanlık and Zangoçlar ve Aynalar (publ.: Plüton Yayın). He is the chief -editor of Corvinus. His work has appeared widely in Turkey.

Tommy Twilite

The Key

when I disappoint you
will you still forgive me
for loving you

and if I throw words at your feet
will you let them fall
without a sound

and if the stones in the river don't move
will you lift them up
smooth and wet

like a cloud you go by
in a cloudless sky
without surface

still I long for the line
that connects us
that hooks you in

and there is something else

there are pieces and parts
on the ground
for you to choose

if you clean them with turpentine
will they once again gleam with purpose
and fly away
like sweet dreams

better not to say
what I really mean by that

because there is no picture of us in the chapel
all of those pictures are gone, gone, gone

and everything is covered with dust
and once again fingertips touch skin

it was that way in the beginning
a taste of sweat
the scent of our being like gear oil and chocolate

if you need it now
I can manifest and come

I was your machine
and you were my master
it could be that way again

if only we could only find the key

Tommy Twilite is an old school troubadour of songs, poems and stories. He is a Lifetime Beat Poet Laureate, founder of the Florence Poets Society, and former editor of the Silkworm annual review. Tommy believes music and poetry can change the world. You can listen to his weekly radio show, The Twilite Poetry Pub on WXOJ valleyfreeradio.org.

J R Turek

Geddylee

I didn't know your name back then,
didn't know if you were a boy or girl
but fell for you the first time I saw you.

My daily route to work took me on
a quasi-main road, several stop signs
and red lights and that's how I found you –
patrolling your fenced-in yard, a busy job,
corner lot kept you busy, barking at walkers,
runners, bikers, and drivers. I slowed down
every time I passed your white ranch with
an inviting front patio and wind chimes
singing from the porch roof, lyric backdrop
to your barks, that were friendly, as if you
were begging passersby to come over,
pet me, play with me, here's my ball,
you could throw it and I'll retrieve it
and we'll do it again, again...

But I couldn't stop and play; I wanted to.
Your mom was on the same schedule as I was
because there you were every weekday morning,
racing back and forth, a colonel issuing orders
to slow down, you're living too fast. Week
after week, seasons of months, I'd slow down,
open the passenger window and call out

“Hey pretty baby!” and you’d respond in kind,
barking and running the length of the property,
turning the corner when I continued on, watching
hoping waiting. Some days, you were waiting
on my commute home. Sitting more, running less
but still gifting me your canine smile.

We did this for years, a cute scruffy mutt sprouts
a grey beard, your gait slows, barks a little gruffer,
but still yearning for a playmate. Grumpy mornings,
you made my day, a cajoling laugh increased
the speed of your tail wagging, always wagging,
even when you were running.

And then one day, nothing. I thought vacation maybe,
they’re away or your mom slept in, but day after day,
you weren’t there. I missed you. My drive became
as onerous as the job I was headed to; eventually I
found a new job, a better one that headed me
in a different direction.

Evening and weekend drives around town, I’d
often detour to pass that quaint white ranch with
Beware of Dog signs posted on the chain link.
No you. I kept you in a secret chamber of my heart,
you, that special dog whose name I didn’t know.
We had four dogs of our own but there was never
a competition for my love and devotion. You
were number five.

I was tempted to ring the bell, finally reveal
our years of clandestine meeting but life got
in the way and I never mustered the courage,
until one day last month, I saw a new puppy
running in your yard, with another dog chasing,
and I was jealous for you for just an instant before
I reveled in the now, my chance to tell your mom,
throwing the ball, though not your ball, about us.

You were there, looking down from doggie heaven,
I know, and grinning your canine smile as we hugged,
shed a few mutual love tears, and I welcomed your
sibling. When I drive by, I still expect to see you,
but I can hear you, welcoming me into your life.
Thank you, Geddylee, for our fur-ever memories.

J R (Judy) Turek, Long Island Poet of the Year; Farmingdale Creative Writing Group Moderator for 29 years; editor, mentor, workshop leader; two pushcart nominations, author of 9 poetry books. The Purple Poet has written a poem a day for over 21 years; she lives on Long Island and collects shoes, dogs, and poems. msjevus@optonline.net

Paulette Turcotte

a Parliament of Old Women

I have lucid visions, write indistinct pages with text, poems, single words, stories told from afterwards and sewn into the chronicles from behind this world, brought into form by the dreams and the lovers of humanity, that holy suffering beast, and in the fields and the woods, in cities, and in the enclaves, in the provinces across this wild country, in the northern territories and the regions, and groups and in the garden patches and allotments, in back yards and in the streets, old women gather.

in this parliament of old women my face is my voice,

from eyes to lips is a thousand years,

my country is not a dead language,

it is genesis intoning verbs outside the lines,

descants, utterances, spells, and chants,

innumerable sounds, howls, reverberations, incantations,

invocations, interchanges, memories, histories reoriented,

mothertonguespeaks, my familiar,

we don't know this language anymore.

my face is a map of the world,

and madness is my mother, an adorned virtue

in a desecrated land.

find me howling obscenities into the dark

in this city of old women,

get your foot off my face,

I will raise the dead.

I come riding the night, the mare,

the hurricane, the wind.

we don't know this language anymore.

Paulette Turcotte is a visionary and outsider poet, artist and author. Her work has been published in numerous presses in print and online. She is editor of Banned Poetry, CDRIS press, co-founder of Split Quotation Press, and is a Pushcart Prize nominee. What the Dead Want, Ekstasis Editions, was published in 2019; SAID OR said, Trainwreck Press, 2021, 6 self-published chapbooks, and 2 non-fiction books, 2006-18, She lives in Victoria, Canada.

J.T. Trigonis

Old '89

Crashed my lightning blue '89 Cavalier into the 1&9
divide after the Giants won Superbowl XLII.

So I wandered the Jersey City underworld, cloud heavy
passed motorcycle hangovers and White Mana

thinking how a lonesome star like mine could get the
moon's attention without police and hospital

lights on my tail to sweep up the busted glass—and
me—off someone else's powdered lines.

Everybody's drunk tonight, Saturn-ringed, speeding
with some sweet heartache wrapped around a

tattooed arm like a worn out Timex or a cheap bomb.
I think about the snapshots of my autopsy haunting

the front page of the *Journal*, my little roadside diversion
loitering the Youtube expanse for Stoned-Age

frat boys with nothing better to do than record my last
minutes for their 15 of fame, my own cheated for a

late night thumbsucker, platinum second mate in heels,
says she's been searching for a strong sailor with an

ashtray heart so she can burn away the last of her regrets.
What else can you say to an offer like that when

you're dizzied off a 12-pack of Bud, lost in the beautiful
car crash beneath the bridges of her eyebrows?

Sure, I tell her. *I'll put out the pain, Love. In both of us.*

(Previously published)

J.T. Trigonis (he/him) is a neon troubadour of the written and spoken word. With the obligatory MFA in poetry from Brooklyn College, his work has appeared in over five dozen journals that have made appearances on the bottom shelf of book stands (as well as online) since 1998.

Kerry Trautman

Going Into Labor on the F Train

An express—no stop till 4th at Washington Square where NYU kids skateboard in the park and desperate poets click-clack-type-write postcard posey for tourists on the spot. Her belly contracted in time to track rumbling. Her fists gripped the chrome pole. A busker busted rhymes against a pawn shop boombox beat track, paused to hold his tip-cup toward her doubled-over hunched shoulders, her glare and groan. *No*, she moaned as her water broke, soaking her skirt, the floor with its smashed Covid mask, and tan-puddled Dunkin cup. *The next stop is 4th Avenue, Washington Square*, the bot-lady announced. Shockwaves clenched back to belly like an ever-tightening elastic sash pull-pull-pulled. *Transfer is available to the B, D, M, A, C and E trains.* She wanted to transfer her body up up and out to fresh air, to shoulders to lug her to help, to a place where Friends of Dorothy fought to reclaim home, brick by yellow brick. *This is an accessible station*. Her breath tidal-waved down, down, diaphragm to uterus, to thighs, down through the train's, grimy floor, to the tracks and the rivulets of brown sludge, the Red Bull can, and rats sniffing a crumpled Big Mac wrapper. *The elevator is located at the north end of the platform*. The train squealed slower, slower, slower still. Ache burrowed through her gut, hips widening, pressure deepening, an ache for the triumph of park and arch and fountain above, and protesters megaphone-ing anti-war, anti-bigotry, anti- anti- over heads of weed vendors, henna tats, and labradoodle frisbees. *This is 4th Avenue, Washington Square*, and the doors whooshed open with a waft of platform heat and echo, and her knees forgot how weight is born, and her ankles how to stabilize a turmoiled thing, and she dropped to the platform, as off-ers off-ed and on-ers on-ed, stepping over the wailing whale of her, calved in half. *Stand clear of the closing doors*. And *bing-bong* the F train rumbled away anew, and by Coney Island, a cord will be cut, the end of the line.

Kerry Trautman is a lifelong Ohioan whose work has appeared in numerous journals and anthologies. Her books are: *Things That Come in Boxes*; *To Have Hoped*; *Artifacts*; *To be Nonchalantly Alive*; *Marilyn: Self-Portrait, Oil on Canvas*; *Unknowable Things*; and *Irregulars.*

Igor Pop Trajkov

Embryo In The Mornings

While brainstorming he struggled to unwrap his diapers.

They were bandages that tightened his waist

so waist wouldn't tear, during the too-hard labors

when he struggled to untangle himself from tired

days and boring thoughts, created in the cradle

of delivery...

The moment of everything that lies ahead has come

Everyone now knows that he must stand alone

The memory of the former cradle has come

Which was completely eroded by the next,

And by the next and the next, who knows which

Next subdued, in space and time,

Arranged initiation for the belief

In the lie and all her children, so that we'll hear
Totally the hymn, formulated in these 9 verses...

And this initiation is over, the patient
awakens in the space lavishly developed in the
time of injustice. The morning is gray,
the child is no longer in him, this'll give high
level to his thoughts and the emotion
arising from the resistance to grayness.
Yet this sloth also knows that the animal
is also a reptile or mammal, it has emotions, joyful
surges, but not that man with outbursts
of strivings. The morning naps have stopped,
the bitter day is now beginning; this man also
knows how much again he will love the child
who is again being reborn in him; the man

himself will develop him with virtues,

while does not cease the terrible echo of

the next initiation, which the death of the child

again foreshadows, not knowing that the greatest

secret is that the child always, yet again

reborns precisely that man, so persistently.

Igor Pop Trajkov is renowned writer and film director from North Macedonia, and multidisciplinary international artist. Very prolific in all literary disciplines. Published in some of the most significant literary magazines, academic journals, winning few prizes for his achievements. Defended his PhD thesis in cultural studies on Faulkner's film adaptations.

Nancy Tolin - The Portable Royal Typewriter

Jack Kerouac's Gift to Neal Cassady

An enterprising John Cassady had an idea
involving his famous father's portable Royal typewriter
The typewriter Allen Ginsberg purchased for Neal Cassady
while he was incarcerated at San Quentin
Jack Kerouac had provided the money for the typewriter
The Beats take care of their own...

In 2005, John approached me with a question
Did I think publishers might be interested
in knowing the last thoughts of his father?
He had access to the typewriter ribbon—if unspooled
the inked ribbon could reveal his father's last thoughts
perhaps uncovering something new

An intriguing question
Transcribing would take time and patience
Inked fabric ribbon would show the keystrokes
Sequence of the letters preserved, but in reverse order
Another challenge for the transcription
Neal Cassady was an icon, a muse
an inspiration for the writers of the Beat Generation
a central figure, but not recognized as a Beat writer

Not knowing what to say
I said I didn't know
Perhaps he should try unspooling a good length
of ribbon and investigate for himself

if the content contained anything
that publishers might value
Another consideration, other people besides his father
may have used the typewriter

My initial thought was perhaps
John was desperate for money
And for the record, I don't know if he ever followed through
and pitched the idea

Decades later, I had a vision
A creative vision embracing magical realism
A view of the Beat Generation and its literary
and cultural accomplishments, good and bad
Kerouac's "burn, burn, burn like fabulous
yellow roman candles exploding like spiders
across the stars..." Imagery so vivid
A complete refusal to accept conformity in the 1950s
A search for meaning, a search for freedom of expression
Searches often fueled by sex, alcohol, and drugs

I envisioned the typewriter ribbon slowly unwinding from
its metal spool, the long black ribbon catching the wind
and fluttering freely, rhythmically, like a streamer
its letters in single file like a long continuous strand of DNA
And somehow, somehow bring in CRISPR to edit and snip
any harmful sequences leading to major mental illnesses
Neal and Jack, at different times in their lives, had been
diagnosed with schizophrenia
They both were alcoholics, and they died in their 40s

What if the Universe had given them another chance
to reenter the world of the Beat Generation
This time without their mental health issues
Would they still be open to the intensity of life?
And be as wonderfully creative?
Would they have treated the women in their lives
with a little more kindness? A little more respect?
Would they be able to "burn, burn, burn," yet
be mindful and practice non-harming—including
not harming themselves?

Would they have grown?
Would they have embraced intimacy?

Would they have found greater meaning in their lives?
Would they have stopped running away?

Nancy Tolin is a California artist and writer (poetry and prose) who exhibits her artwork in nationally juried shows and contributes to newspaper poetry columns and anthologies. Often, at 3:00am, she searches for her mischievous Muse who delights in playing hide-and-seek games in her mind.

Myrtle Thomas

A Pillar of Salt

Life is either light or darkness
politics in church
the dressing of nakedness
the disrobing act of kindness
the cruelty that lies in the heart
gold coins falling from the sky
deals once done in secret rooms
now openly thrown in the faces -
of society.

All of the poor face their destruction
longing for loaves of bread and fishes
wandering through homeless camps
hiding from the iceman whose hands
are as cold as their badge
their eyes like winged ravens
searching for prey.

Why turn your face from a weeping child !
a child who cries for a sandwich and a drink
that child saved from abortion now cries-
for a bed and a bandage
no doctor for the sickness of cruelty
there isn't enough food for the hungry
or the homeless.

Men in stiff suits - their faces painted
in the colors of a woman as the make up runs
down their necks and stains the shirts like
the hearts they carry without compassion
we witness the mean workings of soiled hearts
the exposed selfishness of the wealthy
spit in the faces of the poor.

Will these who have little to nothing become-
as a stalk of wheat dying the fields unharvested ?
could the days become even darker than now !
I doubt your wealth will follow you to the cemetery
for thieves and decay will eat away your riches
leaving you as poor as the ones you find inferior-
the wind will laugh at your demise.

Myrtle Thomas has been published in several poetry journals and has self-published her own poetry. She is a member of ALLpoetry.com under the Penn name BlueBird74. She lives in the USA in a quaint historical town in Indiana. Poetry has been such a grand part of her life , a bandage for her own wounds.

Lily Swarn

Jalam -The drop of life
(Aab E Hayaat)

A minuscule tear drop rolling down damask cheeks

Bringing in its wake a river of peace

Cleansing ,purging hearts with saline waters

The same drop that rolls off a verdant leaf

As a glistening dewdrop reflecting sunshine

In myriad crystalline colours of life

Thirsty birds bathing in scalding summers

Royal tigers lapping up shimmering ponds

Sweaty labourers guzzling from clay' matkas '

Poseidon ,Greek god of waters around the earth

Creates springs with the strike of his trident

Varuna , the Hindu god presides over sky , oceans and water

It's this drop that keeps creation ticking

Each heartbeat pumping crimson blood

Racing in brooks of liquid 'Gulal '

Put it as Ganga jal in a dying man's mouth

Pass it in a tumbler to granny's trembling hands

Or top it over an expensive usquebaugh

Lily Swarn, International Beat Poet Laureate acclaimed, multilingual poet, author, columnist , radio show host, Peace and Humanity Ambassador, has written 9 books in different genres.With over 70 international and national awards, Lily's poetry has been translated into 21 languages

Belinda Subraman

Insomnia

An energetic surge can squeeze the heart
and keep it electrified
urgently awake
all the layers alive
a party within the skin
of juicy confusion.
Sleep seems a bored stranger
listening through ear buds alone.
It seems an untimely death.
A fear of unbeing remains
always alert for sounds
in the silence.

Belinda Subraman, Texas Beat Poet Laureate 2023-2025, is currently working as Managing Editor for BeatLife magazine and editor/publisher for GAS: Poetry, Art and Music. She enjoys collaborating with other poets and artists and has published many of these collaborations on her YouTube channel.

J. Martin Strangeweather

Four Metaphors for Consciousness

In the first metaphor, consciousness is like a clay teapot filled with rainwater. The teapot is the brain, and the rainwater is your mind. The rainwater is most likely polluted. The fire beneath the teapot is the world. The steam coming from the teapot's spout are your thoughts. Your words and deeds flavor the tea.

In the second metaphor, consciousness is like two mirrors facing each other, creating an infinity mirror effect. One of the mirrors is oval, and the other is rectangular. The real yet unreal infinity effect is your mind, and the frames enclosing the mirrors are the limit of your body and world.

In the third metaphor, consciousness is like a triangular crystal prism refracting the light of the sun into a rainbow of ways to color the world. Your brain is the prism, and all the colors are equally vivid manifestations of the transformation of unsullied white light, which is your mind. The colors cannot manifest without the prism, and the prism cannot manifest colors without sunlight.

In the fourth metaphor, consciousness is like a whirlwind touching down upon the earthen plane and gathering up components for its body (in this case perceptions and memories), which appear to give the whirlwind its form, its being, but the things a whirlwind gathers are not the actual essence of the whirlwind—the whirlwind is born of atmospheric forces, to which it eventually becomes re-absorbed.

J. Martin Strangeweather is the Chief Executive Prognosticator for the Santa Ana Literary Association. He is also a poet, novelist, artist, teacher, philosopher, thanatologist, psychopomp, astralnaut, and Dionysian reveler!

Jane SpokenWord

Groovin'

working that groove
that rhythm feeds my soul
I'm feeling like
the music has gone
in circular beatz
no 3/4 time
to shine my words with wonder
to shake my world's thunder
gimme that bass
down and dirty
percuss
my percussion
with nitty gritty
that boom bap rhythm rise me to my feet
syncopated time
synchronized off-beat
pulsing the bottom heat
hypnotized
by
that
4 on the floor
pulling Syncopated Rhythmic Patterns
free-stylin' my flow
my flow
don't you know
I funk my time
modulate my speech
emphasize
improvise
not noise
just twisted lines
rumbling
through my bones
blessing vocal chords
an improvised hum
a syncopated drum
jazzed my will

to swing my vocal sword
wail my word
do you feel it
ancestral beats
rise up in your chest
stirring your rest
testing your resist
where you come from
who you be
you be SOUND
deep enough to weep the moon
sweet enough to kiss the sun
with magic
from 12 bar blues
from time free tunes
to feed my mood
let it
ring
let it sing
let it work that groove

Jane SpokenWord's performances, collaborations and recordings include; Avant-Garde Maestro Cecil Taylor @ the Whitney Museum, Nuyorican Poet Miguel Algarin, Beat poet/founder of the White Panther party John Sinclair, multi-platinum HipHop musician/producer DJ Nastee and her partner in all things Albey onBass. Her books, artwork, audio books and cds have earned praise from poetry and music critics alike. Her credits include: a monthly "Word Jam" series, director of interviews and podcasts for Word City Monthly, Manhattan Neighborhood Network series featuring Poetry & Jazz and co-founder of Abop tv, presenting live online videos pre-youtube.

Megha Sood

Instant Gratification Takes Long on the World Stage

Sometimes, hushed whispers are screams everyone needs to hear.

Sometimes pain takes center stage.

We celebrate the moments of happiness amid shiny angst in our lives.

always smiling for the world in our gilded cage.

Menagerie of ashen hopes and lofty desires—

ready to be devoured by the vulture's eyes and empty gaze.

Leaving your fallow mind to utter confusion instead of clarity,

Sometimes meditation opens doors for utter confusion pocked with endless rage.

Sometimes we are caught in the beauty and the terror of the moment.

An orphan's life framed for a Pulitzer. Instant gratification takes long on the world stage.

Sometimes the strength of a character is judged by the frailty of the moment.

Sometimes we only remember giggles at a funeral, not the sickening pain.

Sometimes stark opposites make the best companions,

Sometimes dark side of the moon takes you to its deepest lair.

Sometimes, even deep conversations don't clear the air.

Sometimes silence screams the loudest—sometimes they just fade.

Sometimes grief thick as a stone sitting atop the chest

gives the grounding we need, so dearest.

Sometimes we exhale the emptiness out of our thin rib cage

to fill us with the divine as we feverishly seek the sincerest.

Megha Sood is an award-winning Asian-American author, poet, editor, and literary activist from New Jersey. Literary Partner with "Life in Quarantine", at Stanford University. She has four poetry collections. Her 900+ works have been featured in print, online journals, public exhibits, anthologies and numerous universities. Her poems and anthology "The Medusa Project" and other works have been selected to be sent to the moon in 2025 as part of the historical LunarCodex Project in collaboration with NASA. Find her at https://linktr.ee/meghasood

Meg Smith

The Lake of Shadows

Rush to me, the whispers of my lovers
as you know them; green foam,
a sweep of the slivers of ice that
covered my friend, and his camera,
and the shouts of his girlfriend.
Such a false spring, that winter was.
Rush to me, the whispers of my least friends,
in the black sky of July, in a young girl's
fragility of confidence. We owned the night waters
because we thought we did.
I return, and return, and my love is myself.
I return, to a shore of stones, a truth
of waves, in a darkening sun.

Meg Smith lives in Lowell, Mass. Her poetry has appeared in *The Cafe Review, Poetry Bay, The Lowell Review, Contemporary Foreign Literature* (Nanjing University in China) and many other publications. She is a 2025 Stanley Kunitz poetry medal nominee. She is author of six poetry books, a member of Lowell Celebrates Kerouac! and creator of Poe in Lowell. She welcomes visits to megsmithwriter.com.

Vera Sirota

Preparing for My First Holy Communion

I sit in the pew. My third-grade classmates assemble, a faithful flock. We are a day away from receiving Eucharist, the body and blood of Christ. Pristine white candles stand at salute, donations from Babtsias packed obediently in envelopes nearby. My uniform's wool skirt abrasive against my thighs. The priest encourages us to ask questions. I'm the only one who raises a hand. These are real questions I have been pondering. I ask earnestly.

Why are we supposed to love God, yet fear him at the same time?

Why can't a woman be Pope?

The priest covers his face with his hands, makes the sign of the cross. His pleading eyes seek reassurance from heaven.

The Byzantine icon of the Virgin flashes a grin.

Vera Sirota is the proud granddaughter of Ukrainian immigrants. Vera serves as the Communications Associate for the Hoboken Historical Museum, where she works alongside Poet in Residence Danny Shot on poetry programming. Her chapbook *We Bow To No One* was the 2024 Chapbook Winner of the Eric Hoffer Award and earned a First Horizon Award for superior work by debut authors. She successfully advocated for a street naming in honor of Janine Pommy Vega with Danny Shot and Yetvart S. Majian in Union City, NJ.

Dr. Ranjana Sharan Sinha

Confessions In Autumn

Shells of regret
burden my shore;
the sanguine sinks
below the horizon
creating a dusky veil
as restless waves surround me:
Gnawing memories
beneath lingering shadows!

Regrets about the time
that flew in vain--
Couldn't collect flowers in spring.
Oh, I might have done something!

Regrets about the hearts
that were hurt by me,
I didn't wish to make them sad,
Nothing more I can add.

Regrets about not spending
more time with loved ones,
I was busy and seldom free,
Hardly got chances to see.

Regrets with a wish

that I had done and

said things differently.

Now I think most intently.

But soon I choose to let go

of the negative emotions and

make peace with my regrets.

Dr. Ranjana Sharan Sinha is a recipient of a number of awards for her poetry, is a poet, author, academic and retd. professor of English. Her poems are included in Postgraduate University Syllabus. Authored and published 09 books in different genres.

Michael Sindler

Akashic

one thin fragile page
of Akashic record

left unread
and undistorted

links now lost
stories untold

how our shared
histories unfolded

the map of being
the map of change

languages/pains
loves/shames

burdens laden
burdens lifted

ashen remembrances
refugees' dreams

map of treasured

memory

last chance to read

now faded away

unasked questions

haunt those bereaved

Michael Sindler

Denver resident and current Beat Poet Laureate of Colorado, Michael Sindler's compositions appear in print and web publications, anthologies, media-bridging projects, and performances. He regularly facilitates workshops and open mics on several platforms.

Jay Simpson

Territorial Torment

Boisterous murmurings tainted trust signature tune delivered unheard

moving backward toward the foreground repercussion's timely retreat

blurred future's science friction programmed affinity's autographed trace

dead in water's elaborate questioning obtuse angles strange resolve

explanation's soul-searching moral decoding dismantled tales

ripped time erratic deadline dimension's disordered certitude

deliver ultimatum unconscionable instruction lay face down cuffed broke

final shutdown coupled appellants stand to face the patriots

multiple quarantines foiled departures luxury liner in parking bay scrupulous attention's flying circus tightrope's insecure testimony

crowded courthouse surrogate's verdict standing room executioner's taunt

return to sender no forwarding address surrender's anonymous stare

Jay Simpson was born in Sydney and now lives in Perth Western Australia. Jay is recently published in 'Voices 2025 Mysticism, Prophecies & Marigolds' - Cold River Press, KtFA (Keeping the Flame Alive) Magazine (2025 Anniversary Edition), New Generation Beats 2024 Anthology, Masticadores, the 2024 Nat'l & Int'l Goddess Anthology, Lothlorien Poetry Journal, Cajun Mutt Press and Alien Buddha Press. Jay is also the featured writer, both nationally and internationally in a number of online magazines and journals as well as other notable publications. She is the Creative Director and Author at her blog Poetry Jay Simpson

Virginia Shreve

Because the Tender Petals

Already the whippoorwill, and the shrill of fox,
and soon, with summer,
the glimmer and spark of fireflies

All of Nature cries
Please! Please! Please!
All of nature cries
Pick me! Pick me! Pick me!

And my greedy insistent heart agrees:
Because reincarnation takes altogether too long
Love me now!

Virginia Shreve lives in the small river town of Collinsville, CT, with husband and dogs, none well-trained, but all good-natured. Her poems have been published in various journals and anthologies, a couple nominated for the Pushcart Prize. Featured as Beat Life's Poet of the Month for July 2025, she was also NBPF's Beat Poet Laureate of CT from 2020-2022, is the current Poet Laureate of Canton, CT, and has just been honored as a Lifetime Beat Poet Laureate by the NBPF.

Danny Shot

Teacher Dreams

(Variations on a Theme)

1.

It's a bad day in the classroom
the students are not paying attention.
Some sit on their desks playing cards
others are actively listening to music.
"Pay attention, you little bastards" I scream
"Listen to me when I'm talking!"
The principal walks in, quietly takes
a seat in the back of the room.
He pulls out a legal pad and furiously starts taking notes.
I regain my composure, speak of the necessity
of proper punctuation.
Just then Marcus pops out of the closet
and screams "Psych!!"
I start yelling again
The students ignore me
The principal keeps taking notes.

2.

I didn't prepare for today's lesson
but I've taught it so many times
I can do it with my eyes closed:
Hamlet, too smart for his own good?
Unfortunately I forgot to wear my pants.

The class is quiet, not wanting to say anything
until Herman shouts out “Yo, Mr. Shot forgot
to wear his pants. Look you can see his dick.”
I look down, embarrassed.
Chaos ensues.

3.
I have decided to re-enter the profession,
in the South Bronx because I want to make a difference.
It’s the first day of school and I’m driving to work
but the roads have changed and I’m lost.
I call in to the office, “ I’m on my way, there’s heavy traffic.”
I circle around over bridges and exit ramps.
Half an hour later I call the office again, “sorry I’m late
but the roads have changed, there’s no way off the highway.”
Half an hour later I call again.
The phone rings and rings.
No one answers.

4.
Ileana, the pretty blonde Russian girl who sits
in the front row is recording me on her cell phone.
I ignore her and go on with the lesson,
“What is Ellison’s metaphorical intent
with the Battle Royale scene?”
The class sits in stupefied silence.
Ileana is adamantly waving her hand.
I gaze in her direction a few seconds too long

“Gotcha,” she says as the class bursts into laughter.

5.

We’re huddled together in the corner
during another shelter in place drill.
Everyone is silent, this is serious business.
Someone farts loudly.
“Wasn’t me,” I immediately advise.
The students smile knowingly.

6.

All is going well, the class is engaged.
The principal’s secretary is at the door
with a note in her hand.
It’s a review of my transcripts.
Turns out I failed gym, or physical education
as the gym teachers like to call it.
I have to return to Dumont High School
to complete the requirements for graduation.
Just then, my alarm goes off
and I rise for another day of school.

Danny Shot’s prose, collected in *Night Bird Flying* was published in February 2025 by Roadside Press. His *WORKS* was published in 2018 and his new collection of poems *The Jersey Slide* is forthcoming (fall 2025) also from CavanKerry Press. Danny is a New Generation Beat Poet Laureate (2024-Lifetime), and Poet in Residence of the Hoboken Historical Museum. More information can be found on his website: dannyshot.com

NilavroNill Shoovro

It Was About Him

It was about Him
It would always be about Him
He was waiting for generations
He tried hard for millenniums
He hoped to evolve around
The minds and the souls
To incarnate everyday

It was about Him
It would always be about Him
I was following Him since long
Like air water fire and earth
I was following Him
From the cradle to the grave, like
The lost shadows forgotten long

It was about Him
It would always be about Him
He himself believed the prophets
He, even tried out every ritual
He followed the leaders, the writers
The singers, the composers, the poets
He followed both scriptures and manifestoes

It was about Him
It would always be about Him
I have seen Him in the lost battlefields
I have seen Him with the revolutionaries
I have seen Him among the dead bodies
I have seen Him to be defeated by the evils
I have seen Him crying aloud in despairs

It was about Him
It would always be about Him
He knew, He was too feeble, too weak
He knew, He was too lonely, too alone
He knew, He was too idealist, too innocent
He had neither the strength nor the knowledge
He had neither the tools nor the instruments

It was about Him
It would always be about Him
I know, He would still try hard for success
I know, He would still wait for the others
I know, He would still dream to evolve
Around the minds around the souls
To incarnate every second!

NilavroNill Shoovro: The author of the poetry collections "**Unsigned Epitaph**" and **"Nude Melodies**" is also the founding editor of the monthly web journal "**Our Poetry Archive**". His poems have been translated in Russian, Romanian, Hungarian, Italian, French, Spanish, German, Polish, Greek, Serbian, Macedonian, Swedish, Portuguese, Albanian, Armenian, Azerbaijani and many other European and Asian languages. Published in various poetry anthologies and journals as well as in websites

Til Kumari Sharma

Harmony of Death:

The death is the ending phenomenon.
So we have tears to the death.
But we do not know the harmony of the death.
We do not know its beauty.
We forget its sublimity.
It is just transformation to make the universe strong.
We are losing in the earth with the death.
Death is another life of span.
It is living in another part.
So do not bring tear in the death.
We have to accept the death easily.
We hope for another life.
We celebrate the death with cultural tears and songs.
Sometimes we weep for the death.
Our illusion of life is harmful.
We are living in illusion and painful life of love.
This is unendurable than the death.
So we have to live with death too.
Death is the gift of the life.
When endurance is much, the death is easy.
So accept the death as your easy friend.
Death is the beauty of the transformation.
It is the endless journey to every being.

It is natural journey of life.
Beauty of end is happiness.
It is the sublimity of life.
The duty of life is only to reach in the death.
Nothing remains silence in the journey.
To endure is much painful.
In that journey, the fake love enters to take profit.
Plural love by one man is never true.
That illusion of love makes me wounded human.
So the death is easier than wounded and deceptive love.
It is so painful journey with wound to walk.
The death becomes harmony than the deceptive love.
So life is journey with endless steps.
Death finishes one journey and begins another one.
It is powerful phenomenon.
It is the journey of human to heaven.
Heaven is unseen.
That heaven or paradise is unseen.
But the myth says that the heaven is really peaceful.
Shining stone manages its facilities.
Shining soil makes the statues.
The beauty inside it surrounds the life and the death equally.
The womb and tomb are made together.
So accept death as the fairy of the life regulation.
The light is furnished there.
Breath is the symbol of consciousness.

It is living entity.

When breath is lost, all lose.

So breath enters in death means it dies.

Then body seems life less.

The body is worthless when breath ends.

Love the soul and secure the body not to be harmed by others.

Love to the life and death.

Love to the worth of life that is about rebirth of winner.

So believe rebirth or form of transformation.

Death is meaningful than wounded life.

Death is the shining combination of the life.

Life is harmonious only in acceptance of death.

Death makes the life worthy and lively.

Death is so precious gift of the nature.

The nature is precious with varieties of transformation.

She is womb with tomb together.

So nature is precious being of the universe.

Nature is the shining jewel of harmony and life.

Wealthy life is to struggle and win.

The precious life is to take long journey with eternal thing.

The life is beautiful only when death keeps away enemies.

Otherwise the people ignore me and my worth.

Love is death too.

Deceptive love is harmful and more dangerous than death.

So death is eternal force of life.

Death is the cloth of wound.

It is shawl of fame too with good deeds.

Death comes with varieties of waves.

It is with varieties of unseen pattern.

So death is powerful than politics.

It is criminal and kind.

It is curious and cruel. Death seems kind to me.

It is dignified eternal entity for me.

Death keeps me in the highest part of eternity.

So death is my bosom mate.

That keeps me alive and strong.

Death is kind fellow to me than the deceptive follower and relatives.

So death is harmonious beauty.

Miss Til Kumari Sharma is a Multi Award Winner in writing from an international area from Paiyun 7- Hile Parbat, Nepal. A featured-poet and a best-selling co author too and is a poet of the World Record Book " HYPERPOEM". She is one of many artists to break a participant record to write a poem about the Eiffel Tower of France. Her World Personality is published in Multiart Magazine from Argentina. She is published as the face of the continent (Cover Page of Asia) in Humanity Magazine. She is made as portrait " Poetic Legend of Asia" by Nigerian Painter and she is world creative hero of LOANI.

Toprak Shams

Bottomless World

Living life by standing still
behind a bull: before a horse

Food, chyle, blood, manure, soil, food
skinned heads and bloody bones
fed from birth with a silver knife

Sewage flows in its channel,
never the same, unlike life's river flow
perhaps for months, perhaps nevermore

A single flash ignites blinding light_
_the haughty lightning of the instant

Sensitive plants sleep six months of the year
Oh please, officer, I'm lost in the woods
a sun born on the title page
sinks beneath the water-shroud

What was that word everyone knew, my form's form?
Pebbles grating against countless gravels
all things without you will ... be, bottomless world
Signs on a white surface: this is a sea-change

breath by breath the sewer ... waited as if preparing

I hear the ruin of all space ... its collapse
darkness shining with a light that light cannot grasp
as it was in the beginning ... so it shall remain

Toprak Shams is a poet & writer. His poems have been translated into Hindi and Persian; It has been published in various anthologies and journals in countries such as America, Germany, Nepal, Spain, Iran, England, Japan, Italy, Australia, France, Sweden, Canada, Poland and the Netherlands.

Mark Saba

What Peg Are You?

Do you stand dumbfounded
browsing the shelves of a warehouse grocery store
as you strain to read the fine print
to discover which version of a piquant salsa

was designed for you?

Do you load the truck at the dock
filling it with cardboard boxes
that house wrapped specimens
of what must be consumed?

Do you discard the wrappers
in a receptacle hidden under the sink?
Do you carry the bin out to the curb
and keep it safe from marauding wildlife?

Are you the one who trucks it away
and dumps it once again
in a concealed location
far from the glittering shops
that stay open all night?

Does the cracking plant feed your family
with a paycheck cut from petroleum plastics
that house your bottle of shampoo?
Do you design the label, enticing us
to wash away the natural oils of your hair?

What about the berries you pick
that get stuffed into stiff containers
so safe on their voyage
to another continent, another season?

What if you stopped to ask a question:
What peg am I in this madness?
How would it be if I removed it
and it all came tumbling down

the way leaves and needles fall every autumn

and, after one year, leave no trace?

Mark Saba's publications include fiction titles *The Shoemaker, Two Novellas: A Luke of All Ages / Fire and Ice*, *Ghost Tracks: Stories of Pittsburgh Past,* and *The Landscapes of Pater.* His poetry collections are *Flowers in the Dark, Calling the Names*, and *Painting a Disappearing Canvas.* His work has appeared widely in literary magazines around the U.S. and abroad. He is also a painter. Please see *marksabawriter.com.*

Submitted by Terri Carrion for Michael Rothenberg

ELEPHANT ON THE ROAD

For David Meltzer

A miniature life hangs from my neck
It could be a bull in a China shop or Ganesh
carried across the world. I will follow you there
and back, David, if you don't mind a little
death in the accompanying vapor
A bandoneón stretches over the horizon
A tango, secret life of dust
The jazz tradition and the tradition it defies
We're going there now because we must
Tilting at windmills in the solar age
How could I confuse you with the last beat crusade?
With your new-worn beard, Fu-Manchu,
cherub face, and all those sticks and legs
and wheels you've got going on for you
as you amble around poetry?
It's another kind of machinery that drops me
on the stage, explains it all away. With you I have
joined a Kabbalistic parade. Along with
the 23 year old alcoholic Iraqi vet,
with skin cancer, memory loss, and post-traumatic
stress syndrome who wants to be a writer
We're on a jet plane together. On our way

back home to Oakland from Victoria, BC
You're high on pills and wine. You tell him
he must write it all down. The apocalypse,
so he doesn't forget what hurt him so badly
Write it down on those scraps of paper he hordes,
the ones he stuffs in his civilian coat pockets
The bloody fragments he can't throw away,
trying to hold it all together. We go on. We go on
And the fuzzy ball of a dog. Your mangy totem
barks at your heels, licks your face. Listens
for his Master's Voice. Is that you, David?
Flight delayed, caught in a tornado in Kansas
A thunderstorm in Oklahoma. A black hole in Utah…
Remember that beautiful white town in the mountains
where you spoke about the beginning and end
with all the other great elephants on the verge of extinction
How you've been herded under the Beat banner
to convince the natives you are not a total lunatic?
Ahh! Those gray-haired ladies adored you. Bark!
Here comes Ziggy, our mascot with his fuzzy balls
and pink nose. Our totem bliss…
Unable to rest, rushing to Sabbath, rushing to gig
A jazz mitzvah on high-wire, wired on the street
outside the sushi restaurant saturated in sake
and hemp, you want to keep partying until dawn
but we've got a plane to catch, David, another

mission to make. That province by the bayou
awaits your singular breath, let's go
Trombones, accordions, fiddles and clarinets…
In New Orleans, they don't know who you are there,
so they don't think about you, but we're making you
known. Gnarly hands on the frets. That giant shoe
Your clear young voice in old chords streaming through
a cosmos of pick-up sticks. Let's go, let's go, David
Let's pick it up from here.

Michael Rothenberg, poet and artist, was editor and publisher of BigBridge.org, co-founder of Poets InNeed, a non-profit assisting poets in crisis, and co-founder, with Terri Carrion, of 100 Thousand Poets for Change. His last, and 31st, book of poetry published before his death was, *In Memory of A Banyan Tree, Poems of the Outside World, 1985-2022,* Lost Horse Press, 2022. Rothenberg left this world on November 21st, 2022.

Charles Rossiter

Rough Times

You fluff the pillows
I'll pour the wine
light a little incense
and get out the candles.
Put the stereo on real low
and watch the room fill up with shadows.
The world gets hard to take sometimes.
Let's stay up late and talk about it.
I'll lick your wounds, you lick mine.

Charles Rossiter, National Endowment for the Arts Fellowship recipient, has been featured on NPR, the Chicago Blues Festival and at the Geraldine Dodge Poetry Festival in NJ. He has traveled the country as 1/3 of 3 Guys from Albany, performance poetry group. He lives and writes in Bennington, VT.

Judy Rosemarin

Nothing Is Everything

We talk about nothings and I love her.

While the world is swirling, churning, turning, screaming and burning

We stay on the surface

And I love her.

Surrounded by gates of avoiding, gripped and girdled by our gag order,

“How tall is the new date?” “How is your back today?”

Nothing of the wider world wildly swirling, crying, turning, changing.

And I love her.

We speak of decorating, instead of differences,

Wedding plans instead of worries,

Assiduously avoiding all aspects of our country’s chaos.

We hide, we skip, we skirt the fears and avoid, for fear of falling.

No talk of the potential of polluted air and poisoned water

That she and I will breathe and drink in the future.

And I love her.

We speak only of sure safe subjects.

“My exams are soon.” “My housekeeper broke a vase.”

Not about worldly matters,

Staying safe in life’s daily chatter.

Nonsense and nothings hold us together.

Decades of love steadily binds and bolsters us

Even as the world grows steadily scarier.

Because.

Because we made a contract.

Don't talk about the serious, scary, chilling stuff.

The alarming and disturbing stuff. The frightening stuff

Because it's too frightening to talk about the frightening stuff.

And this nothing talking remains and repeats,

As we maintain rules and restrictions of careful conversations.

I manage my anguish of not sharing how frightened I am

For I am scared but scared to scare her and Grandmas don't do that.

I don't want that.

And we talk about nothing and I love her.

And sweetly, suddenly nothing becomes everything.

Judy Rosemarin is a co-author of BECOMING AN EXCEPTIONAL EXECUTIVE COACH. She was a contributing weekly columnist for the New York Post. She enjoys rich conversations, gardening and training her soon-to- be- therapy dog, Cookie. Judy lives in Long Beach, New York with an MS in Photography and Journalism, a Masters in Counseling and Social Work and adores her grandchildren.

Linda Rizzo

I'm Telling You Now

What is it
what is it that
makes me move
makes me groove
I'll tell you now
I'll put my finger on it
my finger on the pulse
it's the rhythm
the heartbeat
the groove
is in the heart
of the heartbeat
the beat
the beat goes on
the beat box
the Boxtops
telling me lonely days
are gone
did you write me a letter
Beatle suits
white boots
grass roots
sha la la la
live for today
I wanna hold your hand
I wanna take you higher
I wanna be your dog
I wanna be the black eyelinered
Shangri-Las
the shagged-out

Rod's ooh-la-la's
the purple-hazed
velvet underground
of New York City
my country tis of thee
sweet land of
guitars gently weeping
sweeping
you up in their mystic
anarchistic
strumming
telling their tales
of love
and lust
and loss
being coaxed
coerced
sacred and profane
modulations
and incantations
there are only so many chords
so take one
take the B
or C
or E
or F
take the A train
up or down
or all around this town
black vinyl discs
spinning
a long and low
sultry slow turn
to everything

turn
turn
turn
on the turntable
a needle on the record
like a needle in my arm
slave to the rhythm
addicted to the music
no 12-step
maybe 2-step
dancing the night away
to define love
divine love
it's my
river deep
mountain high
love
of music

I'm telling you now

Linda Rizzo is a native New Yorker, a designer, a DJ, a photographer, and perhaps, a Jedi. She is also an occasional writer. Having had various creative careers, she is apparently entirely right-brained.

Paul Richmond

Gardens

As I stood up
From bending over the garlic
Collecting garlic scapes
To stretch my back

At 73
I am standing in this garden
That I helped create
With my partner

All those years of searching for a partner
All those years I was planting gardens

My mother had a garden
She tried to get me involved
Mostly she wanted to garden
And there I was
So she tried to get me to do things
The only thing I remember
Is I was supposed to be
Throwing the rocks to one side
My awareness of the world around me
Was limited
My vision blurry
I reach down
And the rock
Was a toad
The aliveness in my hand
Had me screech out
On telling my mother

I vaguely recall she was slightly interested
Or believed me
Since earlier I had introduced her
To my imaginary friends

Now 73
I stand in one of the many raised beds
Weeding and trying to reach everything

I hear tires on gravel
My honey is back home

I head to the house
The kitchen
Frying up the garlic scapes
With the eggs and all the other
Delights filling our fridge and shelves

My awareness is less blurred
I am still learning to see
I consciously acknowledge
My gratefulness
And give thanks

Paul Richmond was awarded Beat Poet Laureate by National Beat Poetry Foundation for, MA 2017-2019, USA 2019-2020, & Lifetime 2022. Performs nationally and internationally, solo and with "Do It Now." He has eight books, more info www.humanerrorpublishing.com

Hema Ravi

Creating, Preserving Culture…

"Wedding dessert lay buried deep inside the freezer
for five decades. During a deep cleaning session,
the writing on the tightly wrapped package revealed:

'Do not open until 2018!'

A chunk of wedding cake preserved,
to be shared on their fiftieth anniversary…the sharing
of vows never happened- her better half gone!
Son encouraged Mom to unwrap the aluminum foil,
and let it thaw, pushing aside prejudiced views -

'No concerns, the oldest one is about 161 years old!'

*'Gharchola sarees are cherished family heirlooms
passed down through generations...'* Multi-millionaire
girl's wedding outfit – a 16-panelled ghagra worth
hundreds of crores. Noteworthy, the drape on her shoulder –
her mom's 35-year-old wedding sari.

Connecting with people and places, not just from
the present but also from the past, reveals a world anew.

Sepia-tone photographs, handwritten letters,
crumpled diaries, the scent of old books
bring along infinite sensory pleasures,
greater awareness to rediscover talents,
traditions, customs, and practices…
Such narratives help to establish identities,
core to our very being,
to recognize we're leaves of one gigantic tree –
"Humaniqueness!"

Hema Ravi is a poet, author, reviewer, editor (Efflorescence), and independent researcher.

She is the author of *Joie De Vivre, The Cuckoo Sings Again, Everyday English, and Write Right Handwriting.* As Secretary of Chennai Poets' Circle, she empowers poets to unleash their creative potential effectively.

Tajalla Qureshi

An Ocean's opulence

The waves of embroidered opulence
clinging the sensorus, soulful and symbolic richiness
into his measureless resilience

Queen of wisdom—catches the pulses of beauty
in her appealing appearance and serving duty;
to swathe the wounded veins,

Weave the transparency together as splashes
with occupancy to murmur the blinky bright flashes;
where absences, and blur glances, fully smashes

Regimes over the skies, the clarity in the eyes
Speak swiftly to the free will—magically admires
and classiness clarifies the unheard acquires

They, the luxury of the ocean, the ornament of love
Swing kiss, portraying the untold saga, right above
and there she whispers verses of dazzling doves

Beyond the fickleness, a lengthy long, straight away

their tale that still dwells, into a keen portray

to reveal the fate, that fetches the heart closer

She, the Athena, the glory of trance and elegance

Relishes the Apollo, the gace of the grand ocean

for his preposterous resplendence.

Tajalla Qureshi hails from Pakistan. She captures the feminine essence, exploring chastity, transparency, and magnificence. She bridges eras through phantasmagoric verse. Her unique voice, lyrical language, and profound insights have solidified her position as a leading literary figure in Pakistan and beyond. She crafts mesmerizing poems, thought-provoking columns, and soul-stirring creative pieces that resonate with readers worldwide.

Antonio Pineda

Winter Roses

A Tribute to Friend & Mentor Richard Brautigan

The sun moves backward in the sky.
Naiad, your poisoned embraces
Sought his adventures to die.
For him there are no tomorrows.

Only the perfumed kisses of yesterday,
Exiled to a land of Misty moonlight.
Quoth the prophet of black tomorrow,
Devil's golden arrow in full flight.

Angel Witch, your intoxicating charms
Ordain the thespian to fall from Grace.
Fate Sealed by order of ducal arms.
Spirit Tortured by lance and mace.

The director orders the cameras to roll.
The omniscient surrealist eye illuminating
A Crisis of the dark night of the soul.
Cinema verite the supernatural penetrating.

So the mise en scene is ordained.

The bard writes of broken dreams.

Hollywood Boulevard his soul stained.

Winter Roses fall on the high seas.

Antonio Pineda is a published poet- accomplished film actor - classic rock vocalist and author of the underground novel The Magick Papers- Pineda published articles on Beat Generation artist Michael McClure, Jim Morrison, Richard Brautigan, Ken Kesey, Neal Cassady and occult filmmaker Kenneth Anger in Rock and the Beat Generation

Isis Phoenix

Kite Strings of God

He said—
I don't want to make love to you...
until you know I respect and
appreciate you.

That's when I knew: you came to smother, not ignite.
He mistook restraint for reverence.
I mistook him for a fire.

Welcome, erotic eradicator!
Respect and appreciation
are the scent of compromise—
cold, gas station pizza
with crust like regret—
rubbery, flaccid,
wrong.

Times Square gone dim—
a Zevo light in a dead diner
nobody's cooked in since '92.

A temple of desire can't be built
with drywall and fluorescent lighting.
Don't offer me decency
in place of devotion.

Don't smother eros spark
with measured politeness
and reasonable restraint.

That shit is wine uncorked overnight—
acidic, sour,
a mouthful of disappointment
that thinks it's doing you a favor.

My eros needs unfettered worship,
unfiltered longing.

I want your gaze to burn holes
in my self-doubt,
and your heart to press so deep
I forget I ever needed protection.

I want to be met in my marrow—
eyes molten, spine steel—
as I tremble, open, scream awake.

Want me like tides want the moon—
like the bear waiting at the salmon run,
hunger dripping from its jaws.

Chase my desire
like the wolf after the white-tailed deer,
the beagle, nose-first in a compost heap.

Stalk my shadows
like a snake tasting the air—
tongue flickering for scent,
heat—yes.

Attack my heart with your wanting.
Incinerate our separateness,
even when miles stretch between.

Be so present, so constant,
so utterly here,
I forget how to imagine apart.

And when I unravel—
give me space to stitch myself
back together again
without ever making me doubt
that you stayed.

Be the thunder I can still hear
when the rain has stopped.

The sacred unraveling of
storm-tethered worship—

Love me like you're holding
the kite strings of God
and lightning is coming.

Isis Phoenix (she/her) is a spoken word poet, intimacy coach and performing artist. Her writing has been featured in *Sage Woman, Witches and Pagans, N Magazine, Sensheant Magazine.* She resides in Lisbon Falls, Maine.

Annie-Petrie Sauter

Happiness

That is what is on my mind. How easy it is with just a flip of
The

Wrist--a flick or a twist

Of this or that, it is to feel

(I am in, in that flesh that I wore to bed last night).

A crack, in the box, A mere swerve in the curve of

The cardboard

And all boxes are escapable. Bones spread. Fall apart without

Pain. The claustrophobia of unmet needs crammed into

Wet-paper bags. Melts. Fades. Becomes. Deep into

The irrefutable. Nothing Of a shirt that has sleeves

That are always going to be too short. Not fit

Constrict. Cuts. Won't Help.

My tissue is once again friable. that I why it

is beautiful.

Skin rips. And tears. And Bleeds.

But we know. It stands up for us, or tries

To protect us. Bigger than the big red beat of heat, with

Less celebration.

Still. I dance. Tonight. Outside your car. It is only night, but

Its cool. And Dark. And formal

I am out in it. Naked-in my mind.

I take a steak knife. Separate seams of corrugation

Channels. Through. Our Lives. As we

Run . For the edges. Like the sweet rain that blew in

From my equally corrugated roof. Drip by drip. Wet as sweaty

Love

Like a renegade mermaid.

I feel my way, downstream to the sea

Wet.Frisky. As sea mammals kiss me

Hard. With their full lips. Love

Nipples, and salt.

Always

Salt

Annie Petrie-Sauter Poet/short story writer., First wrote for the underground presses 1960s. chapbook “A Plastic Bag of Red Cells” Bright Hill Press 2009.full length book “When Ice Burns” Local Gems for NBPF. CD Plumbing in Paradise, produced Khari Rashid Hattan. Petrie-Sauter is widely anthologized : Maverick Press, Bright Hill , Great Weather for Media , NYC Inside, NBPF, George Wallace/ Insurgent Imaginations And Sparring Artists She has performed at many venues and speak easies and for herself in bathtub.

Charles Perry Jr./CPMaze

Prescription shot glasses

I love the RUSH...

stop trying to blow out the trick candles in my opera house
stop with the I need to stop with my stop sign smile
stop speeding through school zones of my childish
& maze stop road raging against Self-love saying
::"I'm tired of you questioning my intentions" ::

stop tailgating your washed up wishes
with dirty dishes in Karma's kitchen sink
stop leaving all of your filthy forgive me
fucked up past dirty laundry
inside her washing machine mouth

stop letting fashionable straight-jackets wrap their
:: "its ok I expected you to run away anyways" :: arms around you
& stop taking your straight jacket joints into
pawn shops just to see how much a Holy Bible
& two honest hugs are worth

I am shitty tap water 4 seconds away from being turned into wine
I'm a choke back words chased with a shot of swallow
someone else's pride
a water into wine angry alcoholic drunk Angel I am
always picking sloppy fist fights with lowercase gods

I am a let me borrow a buck Beautiful I
need to pay my low self-esteem
to do something better with its life

a hardly sober Lifetime screaming
at DJ's mixing on the 1's & 2's in heaven

to play my favorite love song

my favorite love song sounds like the filaments
in a flock of firefly's all being turned on at once
my favorite love song was written by Mother
Mary & produced by Mary Magdalene

my favorite love song when sung in Spanish is entitled
"Hijode Puta"

my Tunnel Lights are sponsored by forgotten faces
from all of the women I should've loved
curtain calling up fight or flight from ex's to ex-wife
to ex's kick rocks when you exit stage right

too much mouth to mouth in a suffocating ********
is why I packed up
all of my good
breaths
&

left

left my finding solutions to drinking
problems left my drinking problems
with stronger drinking problems
left my focus focused on

I could give a fuck about what you thinking problems

left my love me love-handle hands

holding closed captioned

coping mechanisms too tight

please heightened 6th sense

don't let me fall in love with someone else(s) Achilles Heel tonight

disobedient even
in the face of death

definitively defiant

I don't play with a full deck

knowing grim reapers by their nicknames is how I show them signs of respect

-you-

-Hijo de Puta-

Charles Daniel Perry Jr, artistically known as **CP Maze**, has a story worthy of the history books. A decorated Marine Corps veteran with a heart full of muse, a mind storm of Marine Corps memories, and an artistic repertoire as well trained and mature as the marine smoldering inside. Rankings of 3rd & 4th in the World for Performance Poetry; his honesty, identity, and creativity have been encoded with that of an outlaw. Currently a student in The University of Houston's Creative Writing Poetry program Contact Info:
cpmaze@gmail.com www.facebooook/cpmaze

www.instagram.com/cpmaze

Adam Gregory Pergament (aka FlowPoetry)

When We Packed Our Trunks

The immensity of the action is the baby screaming out the window in London

and a woman in India

bending over a green

kerosene stove

making chapatis

as a man shines shoes and does somersaults in Soho

by the child who is squatting by the lakeshore unending

as warm snapping turtles

leap to the heavens

and an egret floats lazily

up to a moon that is kissed on the crater that sparkles with mars light

and the boy with the red string

who wanders down hallways

and streets filled with broken glass

and dreams without stopping

danced by a drummer in Guinea who was born with twelve fingers

and decided to walk through the savannah

to catch a wildebeest that kneeled by the water

and looked left for lions

behind the girl who bleed first

on the cream colored leaf of the banana tree that rose

and blossomed at midday

then drooped to the west where a cowboy sat reading

poems of the steppe and the last train from Dallas

and the cow that was roped with a lonely lasso thrown by the hippie who sat smoking in

Kathmandu

and read the Bardo and digested Lao Tzu

who said in 3000 that the yang is in each valley

discovered by the professor who found that the books were reversed

and sat on his secret until he could publish

never heeding the call of the lady in France who was bartered for a necklace of the finest

gold filigree

made by a man whose hands were scorched

when Mrs. O'Leary kicked over the lantern

and Chicago burned

as the cops went running down the street to the paddywagon

built by the sailor who skirted Cape Horn

in the trades of December and froze in his hemp coat and ate ten sardines that were caught

off the coast

of California in July by a boy with a net

who was the fifth of ten children and he liked to stare

at the sun and wade in the water and the sea turtle that hauled herself out of the water

to lay eggs on Galapagos

which were eaten by lizards stuck on Komodo

a fire eating dragon that laughed at the volcano

which enclosed three lakes

one bluer than turquoise

another yellow with sulfur

and the third red with slag

from the iron ore deposit struck into steel by the men from Pittsburgh

who went to the football game and called for 10 beers

from the girl who climbed stairs

she lived down the alley
and was surrounded by lilies that wound round her room
and smelled of talcum dusting the girl
in the jungles of Indonesia after her mandi
her mom sprinkled it on her so she went out to play
in the streets with her boyfriend and wore a new sarong
woven by a witch who lived in Uzbekistan
rode in a mortar and kicked it with a pestle
she carved from pure marble
out of the quarry owned by a lord of the fiefdom in China
during the split from the North
when we packed our trunks and headed down South
a train of 10 servants and a bottle of jade
carved by the Taoist blinded by mercury
and cinnabar powder prescribed by the apothecary
who owned an old text written on a hemp leaf
grown in Dali by the Bai

Adam Gregory Pergament (aka FlowPoetry) is the originator of Lyrical Jam Poetry. He has been selected three times as one of Madison (Wisconsin) Magazine's Best Spoken Word/Poetry Performers and is a three-time finalist for Best Artist in the Annual Madison WI Area Music Awards. He has been awarded two Dane County Arts Grants for his work. He has performed in almost every State in the Union. For more: https://linktr.ee/FlowPoetry

Susanna Peremartoni

Kerouac Jazz

In the backstreet of imagination
in a smoky neon-lit
pub
I merged with your
whiskey-scented breath
to the beats off jazz

what thoughts come to my mind
about you tonight Jack!
Together, we beat the beats
on our knees
exchanging glances from time to time

the chair you where sitting on
squeaked rhythmically,
expanding the music with its sound

it grew louder and louder and now we
stand up
sending the chairs flying

Where are we going Jack?

sounds are mixed with the rhythmic
clapping, the pounding of our feet
on the dirty floorboards
we improvise creaking

the song is not yours

but sometimes it's familiar

a dance
a fire
nothing else
matters

now while dancing, the cool
drops of your sweet calm
our feverish steps

let's dance out of reality, Jack,
while we can!
This jazz is good!

Susanna Peremartoni currently lives in Hungary. She previously worked in Germany as a ceramic assistant. She had exhibitions in Helsinki and Vienna.

She has been published in several places, in American, Australian, Canadian, Hungarian, Italian and English literary magazines.

Several of her books have been published in Hungary. She has also had photo exhibitions since 2020, the last in Vienna. She was a jazz poetry CD manager.

Kevin R. Pennington

obituary for my mother

(for Linda Pennington)

It's almost
Thanksgiving,
almost your
birthday,
but you are
gone, gone, gone
from our lives.

Your ashes,
my father's hands,
remnants linger for
a long moment
as I stand outside
in the pouring rain.

My mind is
a blackbird, flying
in dark stormy skies.

It's the time of year
for leaves to fall
from the trees
and shift from
green to gold,
as flowers
wilt and die,
becoming compost
for next year's
blossoms.

I miss you terribly.
You were a precious
Kansas diamond,
eroded by time and pain.

My grief comes in waves.

Now, Mother,
you are the
scattered seeds
that float by,
lifted by the wind,
dancing in the air
without a care.

Will you ride on
Charon's ferry and
cross the River Styx?
Will Anubis find your
heart worthy, balanced
on the scales like a pharaoh?
Will your energy
pass into the cosmos
for a karmic rebirth?
Will you awaken
in Valhalla and get
drunk with Odin?
or will you rise
to Heaven's pearly
gates, met by
Christ's loving arms?

Now you are the
thorny rose bush

in the front yard,
mythic, beautiful,
burning with
heavenly grace.

Have you
returned
to the dust
from which
humankind
formed?

Does your
phone still ring?
Can I leave
a message
just to hear
your voice
sing?

Will I
see you
again
in my
dreams?

Kevin R. Pennington is a disabled poet living in Shawnee, Oklahoma. He is a mythopoeic poet who is interested in the juncture between technology, science, pop culture, and poetry. Pennington is published in numerous journals that include Sensitive Skin, Alien Buddha Press zines, and The Rust Belt Press Journal. Pennington is the author of one book of poetry, Spacetime Nirvana (Alien Buddha Press), and is a former contributing editor of the Sunflower Collective literary blog.

Yioula Ioannou Patsalidou

I Won't Sleep

Morpheus has forgotten me again
And I will stay awake
groping at memories
from an old diary

I will bring your picture to life
I will remember your every charm
Every grimace of your face
I will detect the tenderness
in your voice amid your merciless
teasing and far off words

You like to tease me
You laughed at my innocence
and inexperience

Once again I won't sleep
And in spirit i will be with you
Scratching at these wounds
open for years

To make them bleed again
and be comforted by the thought of you

I will count the shooting stars

In the starry August sky

and send you wishes

Keep well sweet heart

I will always love you.

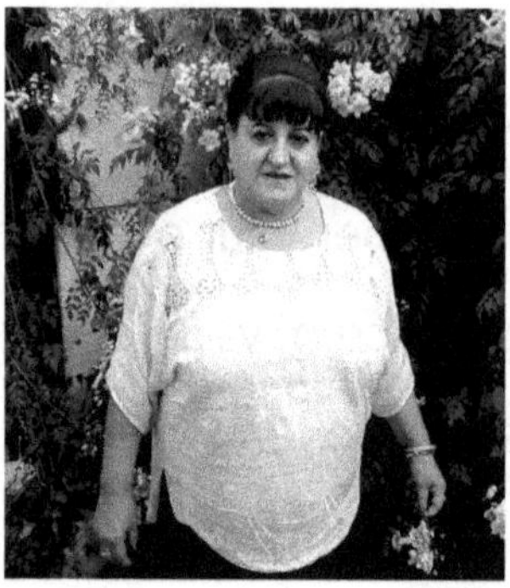

YIOULA IOANNOU PATSALIDOU was born and raised in Avgorou Famaqusta Cyprus. She is a descenta from the historical family of Ioannis Gonemi. She studied in France and she work as radio programs producer . She published six collections and she was awarded many times.

Carlo Parcelli

Aldini (an excerpt)

Blimey Cyril! Four fingers of Gordon's, lad,

Sure as it be said,

I just seen a bloke raised from the dead.

And in such a state I be,

A whiskey neat or ten

Need counsel me where ta begin.

George Forster, what the court say

Most cruel murdered his wife and daughter,

He, the bloke late hanged at Newgate,

Be taken from his place of slaughter

And laid upon a slab.

And this Aldini fella proper probe his face

Wif two bits a copper

What the dead man's jaw began ta twitch,

And one eye flew open and

He bore a frightful grimace.

What this Aldini, son of a bitch,

Rammed a rod

Hard up Ol' Georgie's arse,

And the stiff arched his back
And kicked his legs
And punched his fist
In the Deevil's own defiance.
And may god take me if I lie
But he knelt on the table
And let out a piteous cry,
The same what marched to the scaffold
Be so ashen and frail
A wail deep from the bowels
Of what could only be Hell;
I dare say you heard it in this very pub,
Didn' you now, miles away
If ya had a mind.
And then he spoke, and I say listen close,
For I be a Catholic man
Set in me apostolic ways.
But I'll cross meself and
Loose the tale for another cup,
As I be on the dole and swear
On me mother's grave

As I best recall this be

What Georgie said:

"Suren't me Jane and me wee one,

Louisa, be dead.

But not by my hand,

But Jane, for lack a prospect,

Their lives undone,

What two in the workhouse

Already be blood.

But in that moment

When my neck rake

And I roil at the rope;

When the irony abide as ya thrash

Against this mortal coil

You but hasten it loose,

And all goes dark

And I glimpse Hell,

Devil's and all, and

Don't I be back among the living

With a tale to tell.

But whevver it be god or man

What by such sensation show his hand
At Aldini's this day,
I will not say
As by a mere hangin'
And this force coursin' the prospect
Of fortune what come me way.
So I seek management,
A bloke what can read and cipher
So I not fritter me gift,
Spectacle it be
As part to a pint;
As I be slave to that need
And so with accounts not so keen,
If you know what I mean.
Mind Satan whispered in me ear,
Just as Aldini stuck his appliance up me rear,
Georgie tell all gathered
At this Italian's house and the pub,
Hell be nothing to fear, he say
There be no lack a employ down here
Ushering the damned to and fro,

Stokin' the coals, stirring the stench

What ta bring up the smell;

No belly be full; no throat be quenched

Slimin' the walls of me illgotten hell.

What Dante's be god's finer grading of sin,

The damned be consigned to go

And for a brief moment

By the hand of Aldini's physick

Didn' I peek in?

Carlo Parcelli is a poet desperately clinging to life in the prime nuclear target, Washington DC. He has published 7 collections of poetry and is National & International Beat Poet Laureate for Maryland.

Taylan Onur

Bad Trip Haiku

I held the storm

girdles off it's rocker

like a balloon

Taylan Onur was born in Istanbul on April 4, 1991. InTurkish, he has 3 poetry books, 1 on cinema, 1 on chess, 1 joint anthology (Anatolian Psychedelia - withEşref Ozan Baygın), 1 short story. He has alsotranslated 8 books from English to Turkish. 2 of theseare Hakim Bey, 4 Alfredo Maria Bonanno, 1 Bataille(Solar Anus - Artbook), 1 Japanese Death Poems Anthology (with Erdem Deli), 1 Burroughs (Ghost of Chance). Bad Trip Haiku was recently published in English. He continues to be the editor-in-chief of the onlymagazine in Türkiye that is published in the cyberpunksubgenre of the science fiction genre. Neon NexusMagazine. He continues to translate and produceoriginal works.

Zeynep Saltık Öztürk

Marc Olmsted

Remember, Neeli?

Corso saying he's walked in
on you & Bob S. making it -
"and they had such tiny dicks."
everyone laughing
"That's not true, Gregory, I've got 7 inches"
 Gregory grinning evilly toothless jester -
and wasn't it your tiny North Beach place w/ Ginsey,
Bob Kaufman saying "Bring out the hero*wine*»
eyes burning gleeful (maybe serious)
later a bigger place a party for Buk
you introduced me
Buk drunken like he knew me
 - maybe that 1972 college reading I thought -
"Hank, this is Marc"
Buk's face now sullen
"I thought you were a woman."

Marc Olmsted has appeared in *City Lights Journal, New Directions in Prose & Poetry, New York Quarterly,* The Outlaw Bible of American Poetry and a variety of small presses. He is the author of six collections of poetry, including What Use Am I a Hungry Ghost?, which has an introduction by Allen Ginsberg.

Michael O'Keefe

She

I am enraptured when I think of *her*.

The transcendent delight of her memory is ethereal

And all too brief

She is too perfect for this world

That I could be like her

Even for a moment

Carries me to a place I long for

But have never been

My joy is blunted and killed

By the dull ache of cheated desire

Like Achilles, I am pierced and felled

An arrow of desperation from which I cannot escape

Like Icarus, I flew too close to the sun

scattered, I lie among the feathers and wax

Along with my hope

All forgotten detritus

I yearned to inspire such emotion in her

Knowing I did not

The void at my center filled with disappointment

And the acute understanding of unrequited

Michael O'Keefe is an award-winning poet and novelist from Farmingdale, by way of Brooklyn. His poems have appeared in Vox Poetica, The Raven's Perch, Pulp Metal Magazine, Close 2 The Bone, Manslaughter Review, and Fresh Words. O'Keefe has been featured by The Performance Poets Association and Poetry on the Green in Oceanside. Focusing recently on preparing his novels for publication, O'Keefe has since emerged from the chrysalis and is again writing in verse.

Ron Myers

Paranormalization

Haven't we seen this breaking news
a hundred times before?

I don't know why he chose me
out of all the commuters
on the MTA subway —
the wild-eyed young man
clearly having seen better days
must have taken a wrong turn
in the labyrinth,
encountered his own Minotaur
of trauma and fear
ravaged by meth maybe junk
and lord knows what other
devilishly addictive miracles
of modern chemistry:

I could feel his hot breath:
"Have you seen the papers?!
The aliens are here!
They're alive!"

I took a deep breath
so I could respond with a sound mind
and not react with the fight or flight response
of an overstimulated amygdala…

"...well, yeah, but if that's true,
they've been here a long time—
at least since World War II

when humans became a threat to the entire planet
(our collective unconscious death wish
finding its ultimate expression)—
and probably a lot longer.
But as far as I know,
they haven't done us any harm yet
so I'm going to act like
nothing ever happened. . ."

He looked puzzled by that
and mercifully exited in midtown Manhattan
before I continued to Greenwich Village
for more rational pursuits
of Bohemian ghosts of yesteryear

acting like nothing ever happened…

Ron Myers wrote his first poems at Indiana University in the 1970s. He now serves as NBPF's California Beat Poet Laureate for 2024-2026. His poems have appeared in *The Slant*, *Beatdom, The Brooklyn Rail* and over a dozen anthologies in the U.S., England, France and Italy. His poetry collection, *Power Spots,* will be published summer 2025.

Tom Murphy

Beat Hang Bolinas BO

nasturtium orange flower vines under
eucalyptus stand canopy
ivy long up trunks
dharma bum Tom
I met with Mary

6 Terrace
Richard Brautigan lived
shot his brains out
12 gauge
"Messy, isn't it."
Supposed
Ianthe said, No.

Whalen, Philip baby Zen
Ferlinghetti on the mesa
where he wrote
Francis & Joel
out for a stroll
overlook BO

like
underwear dad
shirtless
on front porch
squatting down
helping
his naked child
ride kiddo bike

speckled fawn & two does
mesa non outlet

BO Gomorrah
SF Sodom
surf fog cypress
because she loves me high

BO
drive against the one way
for parking spot
barbed wire
no line horizon

Beat Hang BO
gothic anarchy
old Chinese woman
ghost
Richard went out
like Papa PopGun
Hemingway

Pelicans glide
rows of waves
surf roar
kayak paddle
Yak board
there's always
an undertow
who or what
to trust

better back up
out of BO
too old too young
Paradiso
speed hump
oars out of lock
w/ Beat Hang BO

Bolinas Community Center
BO CO CE

Food bank Thursday
Banco de alimentos jueves
11:00 am
Elders and disabled
Ancianos y diseapalitdeos
11:00 am
Everyone
Todas
SF Marin
Food Bank

old hippies gathering
for their weekly allotment

thank you

BO

Tom Murphy is a road poet and the 2021-2022 Corpus Christi Poet Laureate and the *Langdon Review*'s 2022 Writer-In-Residence. Murphy's books: *where does love go* (2025), *When I Wear Bob Kaufman's Eyes* (2022), *Snake Woman Moon* (2021), *Pearl* (2020), *American History* (2017), and co-edited *Stone Renga*(2017). He's been published widely in literary journals and has been a featured reader at The Beat Museum, San Francisco tom@tommurphywriter.com https://tommurphywriter.com

MW Murphy

My Halleluiah

I turned myself inside out
for you
Answered yes
when I wanted no
kept smiling
even when
deep inside
it hurt
Trying always to anticipate
each want
each need
of yours
Forgetting
that deep inside
I had my own
aching festering
more and more
gradually growing
stronger stronger
each time unprovoked
you yelled at me

smashed to bits
a treasured coffee table
white-painted infant crib
that once I slept in
a piano stool
I loved to sit on
as passionately
I played the keys
And always always
it was my fault
I was to blame
I was bad
for provoking
your anger so
It was never
ever you
I molded myself
to your whims
your wants
simply because
I was afraid
But even then
it was not good enough
for when you first wanted me

I was me
Now I do not anywhere at all
recognize myself
in the mirror
in the tilt of my head
in the loneliness
of my deep brown eyes
I am not even an echo
of what once I was
And you
you uncaring
you have begun searching
apps & ads
for another innocent
untouched female
to carve out
and lacerate
to your own whims…
I have laid awake
countless times
crying too many tears at night
But now finally
I can rejoice
for at last

I am absolutely me

Free untethered

guardian at last

of my own soul

and wants!

Hallelujah Hallelujah!

I am finally me!

MW Murphy writes both fiction & poetry. She has a piece in the anthology *Gathered Light (*Three O'Clock Press, 2013), and a short story in the anthology *A Shadow Map* (CCM, 2017). Her work has also appeared in two online poetry mags "Breadcrumbs Magazine" (2019), and "Yes Poetry" (2020, 2021), as well as in the "Connecticut Bards Anthology" (2023, 2024) and "We Are Beat" anthologies (2019, 2022, 2023, 2024), and the "CC&D Anthology" (2023, 2024). MW was a "featured poet" at the Rose Room (Webster, MA) in May 2023. She has done readings from her fiction & poetry at various events in bookstores, coffee houses, and parks.

Jessica Moté

Echoes of Pain

Smoke fills the air, a desperate cry echoes
A family's fate, hanging in the balance
Claude's eyes wide with fear, as he witnesses
A horror that will leave a lasting scar

The pirate's sword, a deadly threat
A brother's life, precariously close to ending
Claude's attempt to save, fails miserably
Leaving him helpless, and consumed by grief

The aftermath, a scene of unimaginable pain
A family's future, torn apart by violence
Claude's sobs, a heartbreaking expression
Of the trauma and loss, that he cannot escape

Tears fall, a reflection of his inner turmoil
A young heart, forever changed by the experience
The memory, a haunting presence
A painful reminder, of the fragility of life.

Jessica Moté lives in Bristol, Connecticut. She is very outgoing and loves to have fun. Jessica has been baptized as one of Jehovah's Witnesses for 14 years, and loves her faith which is very dear to her. She has loves to write, read, and draw and has self published four books and is working on her fifth. She also enjoys video editing and the company of animals.

Jacob R. Moses

Compassion Fatigue

Tired of being needed
depleted, antecedent
of a breakdown, I am
exhausted from caring
entirely too much about
being alone for eternity

On too many days I wonder
whether anybody will take
initiative in supporting me
emotionally, especially
on painful anniversaries

I barely got out of bed
nerve wracked, as if
assassinated, sleeping
away the morning, and
on some days, I barely
stay awake until evening

It seems like every crisis
hooks up with a trauma
in the dark back alleys

I lack the bandwidth
to tolerate stress
and that's all I
seem to receive

And on those days
reefer is my remedy

Refer to my enemy:
thy name is empathy

Tired of being needed
when I'm unappreciated
As a bedfellow and zero
Foreplay will transpire

Jacob R. Moses is a poet and spoken word artist from NYC. Publications featuring his work span five continents. He is the author of Grimoire (iiPublishing, 2021), WTF: Writing Through Fascism (Bainbridge Island Press, 2024), and the co-author of Tuesday Night Beats with Douglas G. Cala (Like a blot from the blue, 2025). Jacob (AKA Jack M. Freedman) is a graduate of Southern New Hampshire University with an MA in English and Creative Writing with a concentration in Poetry. In 2024, he was nominated for a Pushcart Prize by New Generation Beat Publications for his poem, "Lottery."

Jared Morningstar

We're Not Going Back

Not to the time
when Ruby Bridges
had to be escorted
into a segregated school
by federal marshals
who protected the six-year-old girl
from the violent stares and screams
of the all-white crowd.
When little Ruby
was forced to suffer
their threats of lynchings,
beatings, and bombings
while learning
to read, to write,
how to be a better American
than those who echoed
the bigoted beliefs
of white supremacy,
while her family prayed
that they had made the right,
selfless choice,
knowing what harm
their child could face
in the name of progress.

To the days of Don't Ask, Don't Tell,
when folks were shamed or worse
if they let their true selves out of closets,
knowing their identities would
never be embraced
by the homophobia, transphobia,
held in the hearts of those

who did not understand
that who we love is not dependent
on another's anatomy,
that no one fits perfectly
within two society generated-genders,
and that no God
who preached acceptance and love
would damn them for
following in His footsteps.

To the not-so-distant past
when it was normalized
that women were introduced
as Mrs. Husband's First and Last Name
or whispered about as old maids,
not good enough for a man
to claim as his prize:
to cook, clean,
or raise babies.
To when women couldn't vote,
when they were demonized if they tried,
to when they weren't
allowed to make financial decisions
or have their own checking accounts,
granted equal pay for equal work
and employment opportunity,
and certainly weren't given
the right to their own bodies,
their own sexuality,
denied by Pro-Lifers
who wanted to control theirs.

And to when children were raised
to look upon the stars and stripes
with romanticism spangled in their eyes,
to believe that our nation

and its history are perfect,
while, also, to accept
that separate-but-equal could be a reality,
that one could be superior to another
based on the colors of their skin,
that those who love differently
were somehow an abomination
in the eyes of their own Creator,
and that women were too emotional
to be trusted with the power to lead,
to have their voices heard,
to have the opportunity to right the wrongs
of the men who oppressed them, failed them,
along with the country they claim to love.

The America they deem great,
the America they wish to return?

Hell no! Hell never again!
We're not going back!

Jared Morningstar is a high school English teacher, a member of the Friends of Theodore Roethke Board of Directors, and a commissioned Kentucky Colonel. He writes about his interests and observations of the world. Morningstar lives in Michigan with his wife and children.

Amanda R. Morningstar

Rebirth: Revisited

(after Jason Isbell's *Foxes in the Snow*)

The secret is,
the first time, you didn't know who you were.
You thought you were just broken,
buried in the rules and reigns,
medicated,
that healing was mantras and grit,
but change was burning it all to the ground.
Rising from the ashes,
you thought you had fate tied around your forearms,
but it had you by the throat.

The secret is,
sometimes, the right thing is easy,
even when you don't want it to be.
Because everything happens the way it should;
because that's how it happened.
It's friction that starts the fire.
It's not the rules; it's the boundaries.

The secret is
finding yourself comes at a cost.
Healing comes in the quiet spaces in between
the roar of the crowd
and you, alone in the spotlight,
a boy and his guitar.
You can't slay all your demons,
only keep the beasts at bay,

and change is the peace you get
when you are meant to be,
not who they think you should become.

The secret is
it's okay to feel sorry for yourself for a little bit,
to say I'm sorry for a little bit,
to grieve your future for a little bit,
to go home for a little bit.
If you've learned you're still alive,
it's okay to be brave.

The secret is,
sometimes, we only lie
because we don't know the truth.
We tolerate the pain of uncertainty
to experience the journey.

Amanda R. Morningstar is a mental health counselor. She uses writing poetry as a way to share her perspectives and as a mean sense of catharsis. Morningstar finds solace in family, science, self-care, and jumping on the bed. She lives in Michigan with her husband, children, and bearded dragon.

CR Montoya

Look Up

We all have choices as we travel through life
we can carry the world like a burden
walk hunched over
lips turned down

Or, we can look up

Look up at the sun
colors of a new day streaking across the sky
look up at the darkened sky with tiny dots twinkling
carrying images of chariots dancing
Cassiopeia reclined in her chair
Orion sword at the ready

Look up at a giant orb
casting white light upon the planet
shadows shimmering in the breeze
ocean waves swaying in moonlight
igniting lovers' embraces

Look up to see an eagle take flight
revealing their breathtaking grace and power
geese in formation
parading discipline and unity

Look up to let snowflakes melt on your face
or gentle rain refreshing your mood

Look up as a rainbow graces the sky
a harbinger of good things

Look up as clouds float past skyscrapers
marvels of both nature and humanity

Look up as jets streak across the sky
held by invisible forces discovered by chance

Look up and breathe in life
fresh and crisp - new each day
full of unique scents
cooling your face
stimulating your senses

Look up when you hear the crack of the bat
see the ball fly as if propelled by rockets
not for the home run
for the ball landing in a child's glove
her smile, lighting up the stadium
lips stretching in pure joy across her face
strangers joining in celebration

Look up and give thanks for life
for love, children's laughter
a day in the sun
a warm place to sleep
being alive, able to experience

Cloudy days will come and pass
if you remember to look up
you will never feel alone

always have reasons to smile

CR Montoya, Papa The Happy Snowman, narrates a series of children's stories by CR Montoya. CR has published children's tales featuring Papa and other characters since 2012. He is actively involved in the Long Island poetry scene and has contributed to anthologies such as Nassau County Voices in Verse, several BardsAnthologies, and others. One of his favorite stories is *Sophie's Unicorn: A Tale of Wonder.* CR enjoys the outdoors and often explores the wooded areas near his home in Long Island, NY.Astronomy is another passion that has inspired some of his work.

Barbara Marie Minney

Dear (I can't say your name without deadnaming myself, but you know who you are)

I was a boy   balanced on the uppermost limbs   echoing the silence

of the leaves   and apple blossoms   star-eyed clouds stare accusatorially

from a teal sky

growing up   way before my time   fed with perfectionism emotionless tears

cataract my eyes   a stoic noose   encircled my neck

I studied textbooks   of porn   fucked my way   through swinging orgies

tried gay sex   straight sex   in-between sex

danced naked around the maypole   spring rain washed me clean

been tied up   tied down   strapped and caned   once asked for a session with a dominatrix

for Christmas   signed in as Huckleberry Hound   to a kink party

loved and hated

sometimes by the same person

I searched for answers   from Jesus   and Satan

enlightenment from Three Dog Night   sorcery from Miles and Trane

Judas a jigsaw puzzle   with pieces missing   a beguine at the end of a rope sanctuary found only   with my face burrowed   in the tits of my soulmate

tear rain drops   cling to salty nipples

I was lost   in winding back alleys   of cognitive dissonance

took medications   faked my way through CBT   tried eTMS

woodpeckers tapping on my head

nearly killed myself twice

no one could find me   not even me

I'm still here   I showed up   I persevered

at the bottom   of the abyss   I found

a fucking beautiful woman

my advice to you is this:

there will be   no celestial feu de joie   no lightning strike

no light bulbs   over our heads   no cartoon balloons telling us what to say

the answers always   lie within ourselves

Barbara Marie Minney, is a transgender woman, award-winning poet, writer, teaching artist, guest reader/editor, and quiet activist. Barbara is the author of four poetry collections: *If There's No Heaven* (2020), the *Poetic Memoir Chapbook Challenge* (2021), *Dance Naked With God (2023)*, and *A Woman in Progress (2024)*. Barbara is a retired attorney and lives with her wife of over 43 years and a menagerie of stuffed animals. Follow Barbara at https://www.barbaramarieminneypoetry.com/.

Joseph D. Milosch

In the Days of My Illness

On this cruise ship, it is easy to embrace
the mournful pity forged by fever and aches.
I hold my bookmark,
a post card of an apartment
in the 19th century,
Norway.
Each wall has three metal bars
that appear to be
a ladder leading nowhere.
Now, my eyes act as if they don't want to
cement this picture
into my memory
as this illness cruises through me.

Each day seems as dark
as the picture of the iron rungs,
securing the inner wall to the outer wall.
I wonder will metal bars
fasten my dreams to memories.

Am I dreaming a memory
of my mother sliding her hand
over my forehead

during winter

when I suffered from mumps.

In my stateroom, reality

disappears like steam

under COVID's hot hand.

Closing Defoe's *Journal of the Plague Year*,

I believe I see my mother,

her face wrinkled with concern.

She leans over me, and I wish

for the tenderness

of her finger tips.

When the sun appears in the window,

I believe I hear it sinking into the North Sea.

Everything is imaginary,

even my mother, offering me

a bowl of chicken soup.

07-22-2023

Joe Milosch has four books of prose and poetry. *A Walk with Breast Cancer* was selected for a San Diego City Library Local Poet Award. His book *Homeplate Was the Heart & Other Stories* was nominated for the American Book Award and the Eric Hoffer, Best Small Press Publication award.

Daniel McTaggart

See Everybody Dancing

I need more to relate to in poetry than old white men
The Koosers and Collinses and Simices
And the Bukowskis are all just omens
Wrinkly portents of things to come

Even the Olivers foretell how much
I'm going to love watching little dogs
Poop in Sakkara-style piles

I need black and brown in my reading
I need yellow and red
I need young and crazy ladies swinging hips
I need to be in bowerys smoking from other than lips

I want to read younger versions of me with a smarter pen
Sitting and sipping on stools towards unattainable Zen

I need to see me dark and privileged
I need to see me light and poor
I need to see a me who uses more than just
Our bits to stop a closing door

Too many rhymes about rain?
They just bring pain
Try stretching out the steam rising from coffee cups
Lower the neckline of a waitress during filling-ups

Try out every human color on her skin
See if the weight of tips in her apron changes
Try being the guy handing out comics at the shop
Do customers look for grease where you touch the covers?
See in the smile wider than your shoulders

I don't dance except in my head
And I see everybody dancing down by the arcade
And I'm every damn person there

I'm the fat guy doing the truffle shuffle
I'm the bombshell blonde in a wet t-shirt
I'm the geek grabbing wads of empty space
I'm the professor lecturing all over the place
I'm the babysitter unbuttoning a blouse
I'm the mountain what thinks it's a mouse

Every young night in poetry is dirty, stinking, and slick
There is no country for old men in the dark

I'm not saying I can't read old men
I'm saying I can't read old
I can't read youngsters who write old

I wish I had the advice to stop writing for old people
My writing would've had much more focus
My pen would've had much more patience
I would've written in the now back then
Instead of mostly back then right now

I can't write about now now because it's all shit
I'll do it later when it's then
I'll stop calling old poets old when really
They've only been young for a very long time
I'll stop seeing colors as a caste when really
Each shade has worn different kinds of weather
I'll stop seeing disparity between genders when really
I'm merely curious to see how all the pieces fit

Then maybe I'll stop seeing poetry as only words

Daniel McTaggart is from Morgantown, WV, and was the Beat Poet Laureate for WV from 2017 to 2019. His poetry has been published in Backbone Mountain Review, amomancies, and Kestrel. His book of poetry, Midnight Muse in a Convenience Store, was published through Venetian Spider Press. He has also published books of his poetry and volumes of his stories and poems related to diners and diner culture and has an upcoming book of sketches concerning dyslexia.

Bob McNeil

Adynaton

It's easier to teach

Pigs hygiene,

Elephants aerobics,

Birds jogging lessons,

And snakes posture

Than make certain racists

Realize they only know

A rivulet's worth of people,

And that's what invalidates

Their ocean-wide evaluations

Of all humanity.

Bob McNeil is a writer, editor, cartoonist, and spoken word artist. Flexible Press published his book composed of essays, illustrations, poems, and stories titled *Compositions on Compassion and Other Emotions*. Proceeds from this work fund the National Alliance to End Homelessness.

Prince A. McNally

Easy Again

for Groovy Lady

I watched in complete silence
as you pushed through the temperament
of your storm.

I have watched you struggle.
I have watched you fall
& crumble to the ground.

I cringed at the sound of your psyche
splattering into a thousand
pieces;

the rawness of your pain
blaring like a trumpet; each note, an echo
of anxiety.

Its breath— reeking of shame, fear, & uncertainty;
taunting you with an ever-persistent mantra;
a looping voice that said:

You're not good enough!
You're not smart enough!
You're not pretty enough!

You're not strong enough!
But I don't believe it, & neither should you.
I have watched you struggle.

I have watched you fall
& crumble to the ground.
I cringed at the sound of your psyche— splattering

into a thousand pieces, succumbing
to the will of your fear. I have watched you rise,
& gather those shattered pieces,

putting yourself together again.
You turned the corner; you turned a deaf ear
to the call of your anxiety.

It may not have been pretty,
but I watched in complete awe
as you faced your storms head-on,

tackling life's most challenging maze—filled with obstacles,
that swallowed you whole / in waves of blue
ocean;

forcing you to sink or swim,
but despite your fear,
you swam those waves.

It wasn't easy watching you struggle
through those heavy bouts of pain, fear,
& uncertainty.

You turned a deaf ear
to the call of your anxiety
at every corner, at every turn;

Until

you could no longer hear
its whispers.
Until
your heart / stopped
racing.

Until
you were able to breathe
easy / again.

Prince A. McNally

A two-time Pushcart Prize & Best of the Net nominee, Prince A. McNally is a teaching & performance poet from Brooklyn, NY, who facilitates workshops utilizing poetry & creative writing as a means of expression & self-discovery. For bookings dm his ig @prince_the poet.

Elizabeth MacDuffie

Fly

(Previously published in Silkworm 17: Bird)

you help a witch
solve a case while watching
the same action unfold on
the television set
in your room at a grand hotel
where you need to do laundry
a friendly woman
in the lobby tells you
the facilities are in the basement
which you simply must see
you get in the elevator
descend and enter
an ordinary laundry room
a door opens into a pastel silk
paradise of tufted hammocks
you want to bring your book
down and read
but the witch needs your help
flying help
you choose whether to be a bird
or a fly by touching the screen
you pick fly then you are

buzzing around the ceiling

you're smaller but not really

a fly in your steampunk fly costume

with propellers at your nipples

you tell your partner about the basement

their disinterest annoys you

a sound engineer in the basement records

the band that's playing upstairs

you sing along

even though you don't like the song

all that much

Elizabeth MacDuffie is founding editor of Meat for Tea: The Valley Review, producer of the Meat for Teacast, and co-runner, with Mark Alan Miller, of Meat for Tea Press. Her poems have most recently been published in Silkworm. She lives and works in Holyoke, Massachusetts.

Barb McCullough

Pharmacy Ho - A Love Poem

Before I was two
thigh, thigh
times two

At six, I sat in a half-circle and read, "Look!"
during shoulder, shoulder
big and little

At seven, I stood in the nation's line
left shoulder, upper and cupped
successfully scarred

At 15, though puberty-late
a forearm sharp and pricked
always proof
and later professional

Meanwhile, portals opened again and again
Russian, Swine, Bird
A, B, C, D bivalent, trivalent

And, at 40 and 50 and 60, recreationally,
thigh and shoulder, the fire

rabies, dengue fever, malaria

riding a nerve headed to foreign parts

At 71, I swan through this Rivertown, past

syringes, blades, dirty needles, Narcon

Hit me one time. Rest. Reload.

Hit me a second time. Rest. Reload.

Now, boost me.

Yeah, just like that.

Keeps me free on the streets.

While **Barb McCullough** sorts through "*What's next?*", you'll find more of what she's been thinking about in *Appalachian* Women *Speak, I Thought I Heard a Cardinal Sing: Ohio's Appalachian Voices, The Red Branch Review, The National/International Goddess Anthology 2023, Untelling: The Hindman Settlement School Literary and Arts Magazine,2024* and The Parkersburg, WV Art Center's Artists' Collaborations, April 2025.

John C. Massett

Bastard Bard

I'm a literary bastard
There is no father to my style of writing
There were a few step-fathers
And you can plainly see them
If you look through the hole in Hemingway's head

Maybe you can grasp my little concepts
By comparing it to all the narcoleptic bullshit
Coming out of the mouths of bourgeois fascists
Not that I have some grand wisdom to expel on you
Some think they have their finger on some lyrical nuclear football

I'm just a character who can string a few stanzas
Into a cerebral idea
Make some images burst in your brains
And I'm labeled king of the dumb-asses
At least I'm on top of the dung heap
Not true in the slightest
I'm stumbling down the heap and
Falling into the White Horse Tavern
You can have your heap

Literary snobs turn up their noses at my couplings
But your work puts me to sleep
Dust off those shitty stanzas
Awake from Rip Van Winkle comas
Trim your communist beards
Rub those anarchist eyes of yours

Make yourself see the exclusionary traps
You led us all into

What am I driving at?
I get scoffed at by pipe smoking gents
And I'm sure a lot of you do too
I'm just a crazy bastard
Roaming around in Literary Limbo
But I don't need final judgments from slugs

I do my dastardly deeds and you do yours
Till Uncle Walt, Dylan Thomas, and Lord Byron
Come back to burn it all to cinders
The smell of sulfur wisps around our faces
And we'll all heed the odiferous elegies
For the closed minded chatterboxes to be silent
And we'll all just smile… and create… and be free

John C. Massett is a writer and poet that has been performing at open mics in the Tri-state area for the past 25 years. In 2003 he self-published a chapbook of poetry called *Procrastinating Ass*. In 2008, with some friends, John started a free literary magazine called *Afterword* which focused on poetry, short story, and art. His latest chapbook *Good Luck with Your Future Endeavors published* (he printed copies) in 2021.

Ángel L. Martínez

Let Your Heart Do That!

Do I hear a vibraphone?
Cool spring day
smells of bonfires
scattering ashes through the air
Sparrow perched, scanning porch festivals
A new pigeon carousel turns
Tiny calliope blares
over loud brass
A piano out of tune
reborn in psychedelic colors!
The least I can do is listen
No more will I miss the sounds
Drums talk
Basslines walk
In a vibration cool enough to fool you
Rhythm is for you to feel!
Whatever you wear,
make sure you can dance in it!
Send a message as far as a cat can sense
You know how away they can smell the plate
Hip cats, for sure!
Meanwhile, check your own speed of sound
What sounds like liberation?

Sing a song about our right to live

Write a Beat poem in any language

And you might not need a translator

Let your heart do that!

Ángel L. Martínez is a New York State Beat Poet Laureate (2024-2026). He has performed in Columbia University, University of Toledo, Auraria Campus (Denver), Yale-Peabody Museum, National Labor College, Brown University, Wayne State University, and Antioch University. He has also performed for the Haymarket Forum with Dennis Brutus. He plays bass guitar with The Arawax and New Haven Improvisers Collective's COMBO NHIC.

Dana Henry Martin

Write This — *after Michael Palmer*

Write this. Sleep evolved before brains. Abscission before leaves. Death before bodies. Teeth before jaws. Goosebumps before skin. Nipples before chests. Sediment before rocks. Lungs before air.

Write this. Annihilation exists. Anhedonia exists. Agraphia exists. Abrogation and assignation exist. Absent-mindedness and anomy. The absorptive qualities of amnesia. Anodynes and apologies and altars and anthrax. Acciaccatura jolting aching ears inside arcane bodies. Write this. The accretive nature of human will that annuls humankind, to say nothing of human kindness, exists. Acid men in rooms filled with acid exist. Apparitions and airlessness and ammo and animal faith and annihilation exist. Write this. Annihilation exists.

Write this. Every night, the honey locust darkens before the sky but after the laccolith. Every morning, those layers of darkness brighten in reverse. Our darkest days are like that, too. Our darkest moods. Our darkest imaginings.

Write this. My mother slit her throat so she could sing. My mother had silt in her throat. My mother slit her own song. My mother sang through her silt.

Write this. You are the meadow now. Meadows have no consequences. One meadow is a courtship display, two a breeding ground, three a carbon sink, four a community. You are a beaver meadow, a fire meadow, a flood meadow, a glacier meadow, an eruption—a meadow ready to be drained, shorn, burned again into existence, into you.

Write this. The sky doesn't protect the body from windblown stones. The sky doesn't jangle with stars. The sky isn't clear when it pours. The sky doesn't carry our prayers like messages on the backs of extinct pigeons. The sky seems blue because, appears black because, appears orange because of our eyes, the limitations of our eyes. The sky only appears. It isn't. The sky isn't at all.

Write this. Poetry is the sky, and the sky can't be owned, and it is infinite, and it doesn't even exist.

Write this. Consider the sky after Krakatoa. Blazing colors drifted for years with the wafting ash cloud. Consider the sky today. You probably haven't unless your sky is a bomb, a dark wash of war, a long wound that won't clot. Edvard Munch said the Krakatoa sky was a flaming sword of blood that slashed open the vault of heaven. What is the Bomb sky?

Write this. A blinding cloud. Write this. That collapsed. Write this. The lungs. Write this. Of hell.

Write this. Have you ever slept with your head in someone's lap until the sun crested the desert's sandstone slopes and you mistook it for God because its light exploded behind your eyelids? Did you believe it was the end of times? Never? Me, neither.

Write this. We sang before we spoke. We dreamed before we woke. We died before we lived. We loathed before we woed. We ran before we walked. We killed before we birthed. We trapped before we hunted. We shot before we aimed. We burned before we smoked. We broke before we mended. We washed before we stained. We soldered before we cut. We soldiered before we warred. We shit before we ate. We slayed before we aped.

Write this. We seeds made the world, made the world, made the world in our image.

Write this. We dwell in an inert past, matter without soul, without wind, without reason. We do not touch our bodies, high treason, but we'll finger your hides. We are not land or sky. We find Elsewheres to be used. We stuff nature in tubes. We snuff light from unholy sources. We are firmament indivisible, concentric spheres, sublunary, noncontorted. We filth and purge. We pluck birds and drown guilt. Write this. We taunt hell every day, tottering on death's pounded roof.

Write this. We must occur.

Dana Henry Martin*'s work has appeared in The Adroit Journal, Barrow Street, Chiron Review, Cider Press Review, FRiGG, Muzzle,New Letters, ONE ART, Rogue Agent, Sheila-Na-Gig, SWWIM, Trampoline, Willow Springs, and other literary journals. Martin's poetry collections include the chapbooks No Sea Here (Moon in the Rye Press, forthcoming), Toward What Is Awful (YesYes Books), In the Space Where I Was (Hyacinth Girl Press), and The Spare Room(Blood Pudding Press).*

Norma Mahns

Mixed Salad

Bent back
Hands cracked
Olive skin
Turned Black
By Blistering
SUN, off 101
Bent back
Steinbeck
Slaving on pages
On "Tortilla Flat"
Viva! Cesar Chavez
Zapata of the Farms
Smudge Pots no longer burn
San Joaquin
Valley – La Colonia
Barrio – Oxnard, Delano
Tulare – Monterey, Kern
Merced – Imperial
Smudge Pots no longer burn

Stanislaus, Santa Barbara

Fresno, King

Modesto, Chico

Redding

Bent back

Steinbeck

Write about

Mixed heritage

In Green, Great

"Salad Bowl of the World"

The Smudge Pots no longer burn…

In Central Valley

Norma Mahns loves to write about her home State California. Currently she lives in Pocahontas, Arkansas. She has had numerous poems published. And has worked all her life as a Peace Advocate.

Marieta Maglas

The Seasons of the Sun

A future reality looms over
our offspring.
Although the sun has yet to scorch us,
the solar spring as
the polar ice caps
continue to diminish.
We know that God is watching over us.
He can observe everything, especially
the confused children who,
when their hearts feel empty,
crave love.
The sun follows
an elliptical path
around another star;
around its blazing core,
creating new spirals.
Meanwhile, the Earth can
swiftly navigate
through the solar hotness; a summer;

360&0&0&0 cyclic summers being
presumably irregularly warmed.

Simultaneously, the liturgical Sundays
take on a concave shape
to broaden thoughts outward
during the green of existence.
On Sunday, the wind can transform into
a force that whips
everything around;
the steps surrounding
the Church of St. Peter,
where the folks gather
to hear the Lord.
At times, the sound of
free crunching
footsteps vanishes into the air,
an air fulfilled with the priest's voice
as he attempts to recall
ancient words
that have been overlooked
for centuries.

Aspiring to ascend
the spiritual mountain of holiness,
the parishioners
have always endeavored
to purify their true selves.
They can become aware of
their uniqueness.

From time to time,
the earth is in
the sun's shadow;
antimatter, comets,
and other celestial objects.

The trees mirror
the shades of darkness
in their woods.
From a seed of self,
the mushroom flourishes there.

Ban Chao Gang Moo reveals their mystery.
Ban Chao Gang Moo is not merely a forest.

People attempt to control

the cataclysms in

the approaching apocalypse;

lacking greenery;

no winters, only endless summers.

Glaciation returns solely in the winter.

A glaciation can freeze

everyone and everything,

especially the wind-tossed,

turbulent waves of the sea—

frozen shadows of existence.

Marieta Maglas resides in France, where she pursues dual careers as a poet and a doctor. The Lothlorien Journal, Three Rooms Press,Verse-Virtual, Silver Birch Press, Kingfisher Poetry, Sparks of Calliope, and others published her poems in anthologies like Near Kin: A Collection of Words and Art Inspired by Octavia Estelle Butler. She is the author of the poetry book entitled Cubic Words. Some of her poems have been translated into Japanese, published in the Journal of Akita International Haiku in Japan, and into Korean, appearing in DiziBooks in South Korea.

Sheila Lowe-Burke

Children of Hope

Oh please! Can we take a moment
A brief respite from this relentless sorrow
Beyond Compassion there remains a Passion
For Peace.

Can you feel it, can't you hear it
The children crying
The endless suffering
And must this be?

What about the Way, the Journey
The heart's delight
The souls adrift beyond the night
Eternal Light, endless verse, infinite universe

The stars, the planets
The measureless worth of all creatures here on earth
Nature sings and roars and screams
Devours and gives birth.

Overcome, angry, numb, grief a constant companion
Hardly able to take action to do something practical
While homeless children, cold and hungry
Thirst for a drop of tearful regret

We daily feast on fearful rations
Of sensational headlines intense and divisive
Defeating all sense of logic and purpose
Or possible outcome of goodness and hope.

Sheer terror and furor crash through the door.
Who will stand strong to protect these children
Such loving eyes see nothing but love.
The highest and best as how it should be.

Not this tremor, trauma,

Dread, fear and hiding, wishing and waiting
Hoping and praying, please go away.

Come back different, better somehow.

Not as one no longer the smiling savior
Fearless leader, esteemed protector
Caring provider, generous benefactor
If ever.

While the children struggle and compete to survive
Scorned, humiliated, ridiculed, rejected
Barely tolerated, scarred, and scared
How can they, how dare they shine?

Yet, what if, perhaps, here are the Ones
Gifted, enlightened, who will overcome
Calling out, crying, singing, shouting
Finding the cure, mesmerizing the world

Achieving the impossible, each has their place
In the disorder of cacophony
The order of harmony and symphony
Let them be encouraged, allowed to flourish

With freedom, truth, and loving support
They provide us laughter, dreams, and joy
Let them blossom, dance, and delight
As children of the future, children of hope.

Sheila Lowe-Burke: appointed one of 50 Most Memorable Women of North America. Michigan Beat Poet Laureate 2024-2026, Cultural Director, Ambassador of Peace, Official Poet of Government of Birland, Ordained Minister, Honorary Doctorate, 2025 Pushcart Prize nominee. Member: Natl & Intnatl Beat Poet Foundation, 100K Poets For Change, Michigan Rock & Roll Hall of Fame. Toured 10 European countries, all of North America.

El Habib Louai

The Cold Eye of the Border Man

For all the clandestine immigrants

It is dusk and the birds
                have found their way home,
needless of a clock, map or sextant,
                safe in their nests with a little brood

Things left behind
against circumstances are visualized
Voices resound in the convolutions of the brain
Curling to reach the ones who left
but they remind themselves of the chasm.

Now you are here
                on the closest border
The border man will fix you
                with the cold eye of a snake
and answer not a word
                He will count you and give you a number
amongst the lucky ones
                who left everything behind:

your scarves, robes,
                dresses and makeup
your silver, gold and bills
                your freshly cut flowers,
your porcelain pots and pets,
                your peevish and discredited gods.

What good is your clinging to unforgotten beauty?
What about the kinsmen and the lost friends?
Your rigorous bonds of blood
with their cold stares and blank faces?
They left your realm with its mundane prerequisites
They are now forming rings and joining hands
in games neither you nor your enemies know.

You said goodbyes and parted ways
                    in your different modern-day Sinais
You left everything behind
                    except your ancestral nightmares
born of Manichean doctrines
                    The border man will fix you with a cold eye,
count you and give you a number
                    You are just now the only lucky one.

El Habib Louai is a Moroccan Amazigh poet, translator, musician, and assistant professor of English at Ibn Zohr University in Agadir, Morocco. Louai has been awarded the Aimee Grunberger scholarship by Naropa University to participate in the Jack Kerouac School of Disembodied Poetics creative writing program. His articles, poems, and Arabic translations of Beat writers have appeared in several literary magazines, journals, and reviews. Louai has published two collections of poems.His Arabic translations include Michael Rothenberg's *Indefinite Detention: A Dog Story*; America, *America: An anthology of the Beat Poetry*; Bob Kaufman's *The Ancient Rain*; Diane di Prima's *Revolutionary Letters* and Giorgio Agamben's *What is an Apparatus and Other Essays*. Louai's *Rotten Wounds Embalmed with Tar* was shortlisted for the Sillerman First Book Prize for African Poetry in 2020.

Karina Guardiola Lopez

This Mirror His Poem

Someone asked,
"When was the last time you saw your father?"
I said,
"This morning—in the mirror",

Fine lines like unfinished stanzas,
wearing his verses on my large cheeks,
his silence in the arch of my brow
and memories behind brown eyes.

Some mornings,
I pause—
look into my reflection
not to fix my face,
but to meet him there.

This mirror is his poem.

Karina Guardiola Lopez is a writer, poet, and educator. Her work has appeared in Press Pause Press, Arts by the People, Acentos Review, Indolent Books, Poetic Pathways, and other publications. She has performed at the Patterson Poetry Festival, New York City Poetry Festival, The National Black Theatre, Nuyorican Poets Cafe and Poetry at the Barn. For more information visit kglopez.com

Mark Lipman

Next Generation Acid Trip, or the Power of Yes
for Hunter S. Thompson

Greetings all you
lords and ladies
kats and kitties
dudes and duchesses
sit down, strap in,
tune in and chill out
we're going for a ride,
a transcendental
journey of the mind,
caught in the vortex
of the American wet dream
and other transactional
experiments, looking back
to where the wave crest
and started to recede,
there was a moment
before the floor
started spinning
that I clearly remember
when we were winning,
the momentum of mass
energy was just there
rolling in our favor,
inevitable as love
on a fine spring day,
it just happens naturally,
no power can defeat
something so strong
as two intertwined together,

yet here we are reminiscing
back on a nostalgic day
when there's still so much
in front of us to do.

This is the moment when
all that fear and loathing
is left on the side of the road,
all the general apathy
that keeps us in place,
it's time to pick up
the reins of life
and ride that beast
into the storm,
to jump around and thunder
and remember what it was like
to play in the rain,
to splash in the puddles
and get our feet wet
to taste of life
while we still live it
and to come out steaming
Wow! on the other end.

Who better than ye,
you wild-eyed dreamers,
disseminators of yawp,
you poets and vixens,
punks and purveyors
of truth and social anxiety.

Who's going to do it if not you?

Who's going to sing

from the mountaintops
of that morning to come
if it's not those of us
with the courage to see it?

Bring on the mountain climbers,
the sky jumpers and deep sea divers
of poetry, all you anarchists
and adrenaline junkies
dancing in the hurricane,
singing your magic and fire
to the air, to the stars
and all that's there behind
lift up your voices
for the time has come…
I tell you… the time has come
… unlike any other seen in an age,
a whole generation of boogie
is coming down on our heads
these are the days
of heroes and villains
and knowing where you stand
the music's playing
and it's time to face it
it's time to connect
to that cosmic spin,
to get back in harmony with nature
to look around at the world that truly is,
and finally say, we can do better…
to make that an action, a cause,
a plan… to create a better world
than what was dumped on us,
one where war finally comes to an end,
yes, that's a demand,

where we invest instead
in lifting up our communities,
improving people's lives instead
of burying them under rubble,
and so much debt
that no one can survive.

If you say that's not poetry,
well, I'll settle for poetic justice any day.

How much better is it anyway
to strive for our dreams,
than to live in their reality?

It's time for a new acid trip
something to slip off those shackles
and open up our minds,
something to help us
read between the lines,
and get hip to the square
jive they've been pulling
right over our eyes
all woolly and shit
making us blind
to humanity
basic dignity
integrity
it's time
to get down
and gritty
with that
to look the mirror
right in the face
and break through the glass

of all that indifference.

All it takes is the Power of Yes

and we can do anything.

Mark Lipman, US Beat Poet Laureate (2024-2025) founder of the press Vagabond, the Vagabond Poetry Bus Tour, the Culver City Book Festival, the Elba Poetry Festival; winner of the 2015 Joe Hill Labor Poetry Award; the 2016 International Latino Book Award and the 2023 L'Alloro di Dante (Dante's Laurel - Italy), a writer, poet, multi-media artist, activist and author of fourteen books, began his career as the writer-in residence at the world famous Shakespeare and Company in Paris, France (2002-2003). He's the host and foreign correspondent for the radio program, Poetry from Around the World for Poets Café on KPFK 90.7FM Los Angeles.

Heller Levinson

Relish

boulder flop tri-part tarantella slap slide slip glide telltale
dazzle fest facet thresh fever flash froth frolic firebrand
contraband in demand wreak reek wreck go crazy deuce
with daisy dash clash flash bash rash no remorse pump a
bone go for tone for belly-ups for balls on fire for jive & jinx &
juice & jelly ply the warehouse skate their skirts skittle their
diddles color

You

tangerine

Heller Levinson's most recent books are*QUERY CABOODLE, SHIFT GRISTLE* (Black Widow Press, 2023), *THE ABYSSAL RECITATIONS* (Concrete Mist Press, 2024), *VALVULAR ASH* (BWP, 2024), *QUERY CABOODLE 2* (Sulfur Editions, 2024), with *CROSSFALL* (BWP) slated for a smmer 2025 release. His book, *LURE* (Black Widow Press, 2022), won the "2022 Big Other Poetry Book Award."

Erine Leigh

Womens' Lot

I'm leading not only my life But the lives of Women before me, Maybe women, all Of eternity.

Then there are the Women came after me, Some of whom are living my life Over again--the controls-- Must we?

Still property, chattel To the forces that be The men in black Holding us back from Mattering, free.

Who pulls the strings? Raises the fist? Holds children hostage? The little ones' lot... What's meant to be?

I rise in the morning, Hope one day to see We do not return To the cage, Eyes closed, So willingly.

Erine Leigh, New Generation Beat Poet Laureate (2025-Lifetime) and State of NH Beat Poet Laureate (2021-2023), lives and writes in Eastport Maine. She is one with nature and the multiverse. Seeking peace, she takes her life one breath at a time.

Kate Lamberg

You long for your own magic

you long for your own magic
yet it's the earth that knows
you've never been
anything but magical

and longs for you
to mirror your purple hue
even in the murkiest of harbours
there you stand ensconced

unaware of the rippling
until salt water bellies up
awakening you from
a salty misconception

caving into
seaweed, nautilus shell-
as birth laboring ceases
at the tiny cry of new life

along the first harbour
you've ever known
immune to harshness
calm as sacred stone

Kate Lamberg - Long Island Beat Poet Laureate. (2019-2021), Reiki Master, Shiatsu/Yogidancer/ musician

Tom Lagasse

Remembering/Returning

Today, I brace for winter's cold. Let me feel this world
warm as the ripening peaches swaying to a summer breeze.

This country's instinct is to suffocate and colonize.
Everything breathes the same air and needs compassion.

History bleeds. Our lives carry forgotten narratives found
in the smell of prairie grasses and the blizzard's cold harshness.

This culture says it's man versus nature because killing allows
taking things that aren't ours. The garden can afford the rabbit's nibble.

One thunderstorm after another; yet the reservoirs are empty. This
life is but a passing cloud or the breath rising from an autumn lake.

Dominion requires husbandry. The divorce rate is high.
Wearing a crown of goldenrod, I, a pagan, dance naked in the field

With rabbits and bees. Prodigal children come back before it is too late.

We'll have soup plus apple pie with ice cream. We'll spare the fatted calf.

Tom Lagasse's poetry has appeared in numerous publications and anthologies. In January, he received the 2025 E. Ethelbert Miller Poetry Prize. He was a 2024 Artist in Residence at the Edwin Way Teale House at Trail Wood. He currently serves as the Poet Laureate of Bristol, CT.

Antonia Alexandra Klimenko

July

I like you July!
I like your sunny, yellow, bright and sticky
step-right-up-tell-ya-what-I'm-gonna-do days.
Your roll-out-the-sidewalk, cotton candy, popcorn-vendor,
hot-dogs-in-the-mustard, roll-in-the-hay-days of summer.

I like you July!
I like your squeaky high-heeled red patent-leather voice
with those ridiculously low-slung trombone-hips
that glide into sound.

How you had Manhattan trembling!
How the buildings swayed and collapsed at your feet
as broiling streets dove into the Hudson
And the jazz-hot dreams melted like ice cream cones
dripping from the bent lamppost
that once enshrined you and your throng.

I like you July.
I like the red and white and blue of you,
the north, the south,
the black and blue of you
and your gum-chewing tis-of-me humanity
with their *roll-of-the-drum-eyes*
with their hot air balloons
that float on empty strings

in the sky.

I like you July.

I like your fireworks in the ignorant dark.

How you once tried to bribe the stars to shine less brightly

because you couldn't pay your light bill.

And most of all, I especially like, July,

the way you leave me cold with your song and dance.

How I will never bother to look for you in a café

or ask you why

you pawned your soul

for a ride

on the Ferris-wheel

in June.

I love you, July!

Antonia Alexandra Klimenko is the Writer/Poet in Residence for The Creative Process and the Poet in Residence for SpokenWord Paris. A nominee for the Pushcart Prize, The Best of the Net, and a former San Francisco Poetry Slam Champion, she is widely published. Her work has appeared in (among others) *Jazz and Literature, XXI Century World Literature*(which she represents France) *and Maintenant : Journal of Contemporary Dada Writing and Art* archived at New York's Museum of Modern Art. Her selected poems *On the Way to Invisible* was recently published by The Opiate Books and is now available. Her selected poems *The Lookintg Glass* is forthcoming later this year.

Debbie Tosun Kilday

Dream Warrior
For Ginsberg & Kerouac

I'm a dream warrior
With sympathetic tendencies
Empathetic yet …
Just like Kerouac
Searching for meaning
For a more authentic way of life

Take care of my genuine heart
It's like a delicate flower
That blooms when nurtured
Love it daily to keep it thriving

I'll give you my all
Without reservations

At times I might escape to realms
With natural environments
Hidden from spying eyes

I sometimes think of Ginsberg
It was so long ago
We practiced Tai Chi together
A moving meditation
He liked that I wasn't a big talker
That he could just be himself
Relaxing, practicing in silence
But at the same time
If he wanted company
I offered conversation

A friend

His words and advice

I'll always respect and cherish

He was wise to the world and its sorrows

I think of the complexities of life

And its meanings

I'm not a stranger to sorrows

Instead I move forward

Always evolving

Beyond Beat

Open to change

But grounded in the idea

That life is for living

Creating peace & joy

Finding happiness and love

Debbie Tosun Kilday is a Beat Poet, writer, award winning author of books, short stories, poetry. She is founder/owner/CEO of the National Beat Poetry Foundation, Inc., its Festivals, New Generation Beat Publications and BeatLife magazine. She was named a Connecticut Arts Hero award recipient, is a nature photographer, multimedia artist and owner of Kilday Krafts. Debbie is a Connecticut, USA native and resident.

Patti Barker Kierys

The Pain of Loss

My heart is weeping in pain
how can it be that you are gone
it can't be a dream - it's a nightmare
for I feel nothing but emptiness

Will I ever feel without pain
when will the healing begin
help me to let go of the anger
I want to feel joy again

Let the sadness melt away
without guilt of being alive
joy and love was our life
before you left me and died

I scream out in pain
why did you leave me
I would have helped you
why couldn't you stay

If I smile or laugh
guilt washes over me
for being happy again

and you are not here to

smile and laugh with me

All tell me it gets better

maybe tomorrow – not today

the pain grips my heart

each and everyday

I know you are gone forever

but always will you remain

with memories and love

I carry in my heart

till we meet again

I LOVE YOU

Patti Barker Kierys is a woman of many interests. She is an award-winning artist, Reiki Master Teacher, author, poet and photographer. Her creative passion and spiritual inspiration can be seen in her poems, paintings, collage, photography and inspirational messages. She writes articles for the international organization Reiki Rays. Upon retiring after 50 years in law, a surprising passion arose. She began writing poetry and continues to enjoy it to this day. She can be reached at pmkierys@att.net and on Facebook - Patti Barker Kierys

Joe Kidd

Mother Church

this day be your day, I remove my vestments
your beauty reigns high above the mountains
born of your flesh, I carry your fire
relieved of the pain of yesterday's error
to you I cry out from the streets of sorrow
heroic are those who engage under your flag
waving and brandishing their lectures forbidden
the cutting blade, a sharpened tongue
awakened in the morning in the hour of redemption
gravity failing in its attempt to subdue

oh dear mother, you have bathed me in your glory
raised me high above the storm
no evidence left in the unblemished soil
as I sink into the depths of your grand cathedra
you have now chosen me as your favorite son
child of torture and loving communion
here at the border I close my eyes
to the invisible truth of the silent sonata
and reach out for the untouchable projectile magna
the wound that it leaves is the living proof

this is what you have taught me
this is what I have learned
the water has broken, the lava flows
freedom unleashed and uncontrolled
circulation required by law

I never knew you were so fragile
I was unaware of my own density
the nesting bird in its sanctuary
the final act of hope and faith
you have restored life to my body and soul
I exist in the house of your benevolence
beautiful mother adorned in red
my hand shakes as I clutch the parchment
the ink and the blood, a tender cocktail
bleeds my confession from the deepest ocean
my midnight journey, a premonition
a wager against eternity
wrapped and bound in the cast of possession
a gift of love and a life fulfilled

I have sat at your table and drank your wine
broken the bread dipped in chrism oil
performed my penance, lifted up my sacrifice
you, most worthy and gracious flower
pressed me tight against your bosom
covered my bones in your colorful blanket
massaged my heart and washed my hair
in the light of heaven and earth as one

now in this hour of romantic seclusion
passionate desires falling like rain
the mound of Venus, the moons of Mars
hide in the light of the towering dome
the rotating entrance to the honeycomb

I write this from deep within high walls
the doorway open to the world outside
the pillars rise above the floor, as I step out into the light
I shall share this fruit with the brave among you
who cherish the loneliness of solitude
yet it is not myself who stands alone
but the demon hiding beneath this flesh
sequestered are the sisters of mercy
and there they shall dwell as the wars rage on
I hide them from the accuser's judgment
beneath a cloak of solemn assurance

mother stands up and walks to the kitchen
the hymn of the holy meal on her breath
blesses the bread and the bleating lamb
the blood and the water becomes the wine

do not fear, her love is harmless and I will keep you to my heart
and I will dance you across the river
that separates the light and shadow
and holds the tide of the executioner
the green and gold and red and black
where I will kiss the part that hurts
the part that quivers when revealed
mother waits below the surface
she will lay her hands on you
answer each question that you set forth
mark each step each mile each highway

the wind may rush and bend the trees

the comets burn holes in the fabric of time
the nightmares turn in upon themselves
our vision cast on far horizons
we shall wear the mask that covers our soul
our secret identification card
are you old enough to enter paradise
yes, we have felt it's heat once or twice before
hungry for love and dressed to kill
tonight I take you home to mother

Joe Kidd: author The Invisible Waterhole and Digging Underground/Portrait of a Beat Poet Laureate. Beat Poet Laureate 2022-2024, Cultural Director, Ambassador of Peace, Official Poet of Government of Birland, Honorary Doctorate, 2025 Pushcart Prize nominee. Member: Natl & Intnatl Beat Poet Foundation, 100K Poets For Change, Intnatl Singer/Songwriter Assoc, Michigan Rock & Roll HoF. Toured 10 European countries, N. America.

Enes Kaynakci

(translated from Turkish by Berkay Adanali)
a prayer to turn to the paper

to remember how to speak and listen

they don't know how productive our home is
with bone tools we forged ourselves from grief
tangled in our vines until we learned how to fall
hair unraveled,
poured out of ourselves again and again

since this is a prayer, may my bird's wings spread
the freedom of my heart doesn't weigh on my mind
free from all manners of scale,
I'm a city and its beast
my rivers wash my streets every night
all my doors are open wide because
the embers inside and the flames outside are one
while everyone's a witness to the fire

Our funeral will be held after the noon prayer at Darıca Zoo.
It will be an open-bar event.
Don't ya bring your kids or anything!
After the Eid prayer, a couple spliffs,
munchies with sacrificial meat tonight,
Workers of the world, unite!

with flatbreads finessed from the local ethnic grocery store,

a potato, two eggs, a lot of onions and seasoning,
i will crack and eat your eggs,
dar geldi bana Ankara.

Including the price charts for the morning-after pill,
The dramatic statistics of love, that's to say,
how will we split the leftover condoms, my beloved?

I'm the trickster of my sorrow,
that I hide even from my own gaze.
I bear the stupidity of having accepted the fact that
the things I laugh at aren't actually that funny.

This is a forest where jinns
from the Middle East connect via VPN
"I'd rather have horoscope thanIslam
I'm A7med but you can call me Abu"

The Reich Minister of Propaganda and I
are hocking the same loogies as old Herodotus.
I've returned from my cave in the Alps.
Cover me! Cover me too!

Mom and dad's always been a joke,
I am all that is left from my family.
Wherever I grabbed my feelings, I said, it's poetry.

SheikhGPT, remind me
– what was I feeling last time?

Oh SheikhGPT, you know me well,
what must I do to sustain myself?
And, SheikhGPT, who will defend TUSAŞ?
And from whom?

Alef, Lam, Meme.
qol a3ozo berab el nas
malek el nas elahy el nas
been spendin' most their lives
livin' in a gangsta's paradise

The most devoted disciples
of the most complete lie.
Oh decency, what a loose,
helter-skelter veil you are.

(Snorrrtt) A7a neek. Necesito cerveza.
A gimbal locked onto the Staff of Moses,
a vibrating tongue piercing.
Maybe it'll pass if I drink enough.
I kept beating my meat with the
blood of the mosquito that walked in on me.

I belong to my tongue and not my government
– the buttons are English though

abstract islamism, the first spiritual Bektashi experiment with European characteristics, Zaphod at the pavyon, intergalactic and looking for a brawl

or a fashion designer flipping through books of fiqh

I feel like an idle explorer in *Age of Empires*,

I miss myself

Enes Kaynakci

Born in Ankara in 2000, she sees myth as the freest form of expression, from shamanic rituals to Instagram reels. Her Turkish poetry embodies a cultural nomad, wandering the steppes of human experience. She publishes in fanzines, performs across Turkey, and blends poetry with interactive audiovisual rituals.

Eliot Katz

Death and War

On the last car of a late night N train
I asked Death how it managed
to move so quickly
during wars.

"I'm not sure why," Death answered,
"but ever since Hiroshima
my skates glide faster
over the cool Earth."

I asked whether it was possible
to tell the difference
between a civilian
and a young draftee.

"No difference."

I said from my own perspective
there was at least something different
about a playful child
struck by stray cluster bomb.

Death glared between my eyes.

I debated with Death about the merits
of a bullet, a car crash, & a baseball bat--

It confessed the first case
of pediatric AIDS

had almost bounced back & shocked Death
to death.

Approaching the last stop, I asked
whether it ever thought,
despite a difficult economy,
to look for an easier job.

Death laughed & pointed to the front page
of today's *New York Times*.
"Watch your step, E. Katz,
but don't make it obvious."

Eliot Katz - Called "another classic New Jersey bard" by Allen Ginsberg, **Eliot Katz** is the author of seven books of poetry, and a prose book, *The Poetry and Politics of Allen Ginsberg*. In 2024, Eliot was named a lifetime New Generation Beat Poet Laureate by the National Beat Poetry Foundation. Katz, whose late mother was a Holocaust survivor, has worked for many years as an activist for a wide range of peace and social-justice causes. He lives in Hoboken, NJ and his website is at www.eliotkatzpoetry.com.

Karlostheunhappy

A Heaven Of Trees

and when you finish school
go wander in the summering;
linger
in bookstores &
drink-in the mind marauders

reinvent yr soul if you must
take a last dance w/the old you
& build a new geranium soul

then drive the road of open skies
and love like gold evening
drift under the tonic of trees

and if there are no trees
then go make yr own shimmering
yr own tender mist

and, when yr halfway thru
step thru the gateless gate
discard all them clunking heavy chains gathered about yr ankles
for there is no goodbye
only now

so travel light in the light

and

when yr finally done

relax:

yr the brilliant nothing of

everything

Karlostheunhappy

gloomyforpleasure.com, facebook.com/karlostheunhappy

2022-2023 International Beat Poet Laureate (England)

OBLIVION: 200 Seasons of Pain & Magic

FLOWERS OF THE LITTER: (poetry of and for people living on the streets) with Mimi German

AFTER HOURS: a slimline collection from the bar

HIGH RISE: Brutalist Poetry, GLOW: City at Night poetry

COMING SOON: BEAT SURREAL: annual no.1

BEAT IN BIG SUR / BEAT IN BERLIN: Beat travelogues
FLUX: the turning leaves

Strider Marcus Jones

Hopper's Ladies

you stay and grow

more mysterioso

but familiar

in my interior-

with voices peeled

full of field

of fruiting orange trees

fertile to orchard breeze

soaked in summer rains

so each refrain all remains.

not afraid of contrast,

closed and opened in the past

and present, this isolation of Hopper's ladies,

sat, thinking in and out of ifs and maybes

in a diner, reading on a chair or bed

knowing what wants to be said

to someone

who is coming or gone-

such subsidence

into silence

is a unilateral curve

of moments

and movements

that swerve

a straight lifetime

to independence

in dependence

touching sublime

rich roots

then ripe fruits.

we share their flesh and flutes

in ribosomes and delicious shoots

that release love-

no, not just the fingered glove

to wear

and curl up with in a chair,

but lovingkindness

cloaked in timeless

density and tone

in settled loam-

beyond lonely apartments in skyscrapers

and empty newspapers,

or small-town life

gutting you with a gossips knife.

Strider Marcus Jones – is a poet, law graduate and former civil servant from Salford, England with proud Celtic roots in Ireland and Wales. He is the editor and publisher of Lothlorien Poetry Journal https://lothlorienpoetryjournal.blogspot.com/. A member of The Poetry Society, nominated for the Pushcart Prize x3 and Best of the Net x3, his five published books of poetry https://stridermarcusjonespoetry.wordpress.com/ reveal a maverick, moving between cities, playing his saxophone in smoky rooms.

Catherine Katey Johns

Blackhawk Downer

Why didn't they see
radar green, glowing bright,
what profoundly impaled
with the pilot's last screaming
whose broad flames fill the sky
with the perilous flight
the approach was a go
33's lights brightly beam.
But the Blackhawk's still there
the plane bursting in air
in the doom where it happened
the controllers gasp and stare

on board stars were just eleven
and would remain so forever
in the cold Potomac deep
where they all went to sleep.

Catherine Katey Johnson - Award-winning writer from Cushing, OK. Her poems are in dozens of anthologies and three of her own collections. MAGNUM FARCE, her spoof, was a Semifinalist in the Diverse Writers Outreach, 2025 Santa Barbara Intl Screenplay Awards. Catherine Katey Johnson - IMDb

*This poem, "Blackhawk Downer"was performed live at the annual Woody Guthrie Festival Poetry event, day 1, inside Rodeo Cinema, Stockyards District, Oklahoma City, OK, July 11, 2025.

Doc Janning

Changes

In the perigee of day
amid subtle changes
from dusk and twilight

and Earth's quotidian spin

dark touches down at Midnight
in mazarine majesty

Full Moon lifts
and the sky
the sky
sparkles with stars

'Neath this ancient tapestry
Gaia breathes
in gentle zephyrs
luxuriating
in lingering warmth
We lie
in fields of wonder
absorbing
the ambience of the night

And it imbrues and imbues us
with peace

Doc Janning is the 82 year-old Inaugural Poet Laureate of The City of South Euclid, Ohio, and Third Poet Laureate of Cuyahoga County, Ohio. He has had poems included in 36 anthologies and many other publications. His first book of poetry, “Before Today ∞ Beyond Tomorrow, Poems from the Multiverse”, was published by Venetian Spider Press, on November 27, 2023 and includes two poems nominated for a Pushcart Prize.

Dane Ince

Luna

In the cold and lonely everywhere many traveled in only their orbit

Never to meet the smile of another traveler...

It was Luna's lot

Quotidian

The time scale of eons is too meager to count

Residing in the realm of the exalted

You are my Luna

Showing me the damage done

The crash of debris

Illuminating night face

Lighting shining down on me

I am just man reaching up to you

With my hand

Wishing I could stroke your cheek

And you do not know I am here

Lunatic is what I hear them shout…

In this dream

I am inside you

I feel your soft moans

I am climbing up

You Miwok maiden

I am driven

Compelled to complete the journey

Into my heart I am called

By you

Oku

To give up

Hidden

Leave it on the table

Around and around

Spinning

Kurokuro

At the top

On the real and hard mountain top

I rest on rocks and dirt

And watch

You travel

Far away from

My reach

You are exalted in your sway

In this private moment

Deep in night silence

Twinkle of the velvet vault

Our love concealed

Deeply shared between us

Down below the thirty-six villages

People sleeping dreaming

Some of love as grand as this

They leave it behind

On waking

They find their own way

To say Okay

In a cute and sweet tone

Goodbye for now

Travel across the border

You are my Luna

Showing me the damage done

The crash of debris

Illuminating night face

Lighting shining down on me

Dane Ince born inTexas went to Berkeley, California to study art. He resides sheltering in place in San Francisco. William S. Burroughs and South American writer Jorge Luis Borges are some of his favorites. He is on the Beat-dada spectrum between Marcel Duchamp and Andrew Goldsworthy. Dane was named California Beat Poet Laureate (2022-2024)

Amie Hyson

Disquiet Among the Muses

There is a disquiet among the
would-be muses who,
choose not to be amused
by the general dis~ease
of these unsettling days.

Those who choose to
disobey any inaugural order
of the day, to remain dedicated
to authentic freedom…

unwilling to concede to patriarchy,
to papal law, to being defined by
narrow minds, possessed by
deep pockets lined with voracity,
hateful hearts & filled with
spiteful intentions
at every juncture.

There is a disquiet among the
would be muses
who choose not to be amused
by abuse of power, 11th hour pardons
nor signs of oligarchy taking over any
remaining guise of democracy
we the people once knew.

No, the muses will not be dissuaded
are far from amused,
& never to be defeated as
we choose to refuse to
give in to the inhumane ways
of these disenchanted days.

For, if history is to
not be repeated
on the muses watch,
we must refuse to participate
in their abject acts of insanity
as we continue to bear witness
to all that transpires, while
giving voice to the voiceless,
words of hope to the tired &
commit to a willingness to
speak these inconvenient truths
as required.

There is indeed, a disquiet
among the muses, who
choose to continue to fight
for just, right & true within
this T-attered red white & blue

Amie Hyson lives in Western MA, where an encouraging, vibrant & wonderfully welcoming spoken word community, she has been writing & performing her poetry since 2016. She began facilitating creative writing workshops for women in 2017 and has led numerous workshops in her community since. During the pandemic she began offering online co-ed "Writing Your Recovery" workshops, which continue weekly. Amie's work appears in several anthologies & she hopes to publish her first collection soon.

Munsif Husami

Dirty Magazines Ruin Lives

A comedian I know killed his sold-out Carnegie Hall set
months ago.

But one of his punches still feels sore -

"I've got a solution to gun violence" he says.

"Make all guns usable only

when you quote the 2nd amendment

in its entirety."

Sure, there's a joke in here

about literacy and gun violence having

an inverse relationship -

but when you have Yale lawyers

and Harvard-bred Senators fighting

to sell miniaturized howitzers

capable of blowing apart a parent's life,

a school's calm or a city's peace of mind,

then I wonder if the true culprits

are those who can't read

or the ones in suits that vote

for this madness because

it secures their blood money.

The only corporations both parties will
not fellate is the one
that doesn't pay them
to do it -
Feeding an addiction to violence is so profitable,
that they frame human safety as a problem
for the bottom line.

The only point I will make here, respectfully, is this -
Fuck your AR-15s
fuck your Glocks
and fuck your thoughts and prayers too.
When the same nuts that came for Newtown,
came for Marjorie Stoneman Douglas,
came for Las Vegas,
came for Virginia Tech,
when the same nuts come for you,
don't say common sense didn't warn you.
don't say "I wish the 2nd
Amendment wrote about bad guys with guns too."

Munsif Husami featured as a poet on the PBS documentary 'Voices in The Garden – A Midsummer Night's Dream' which was released in 2025. He writes about identity, mental health, immigration, social issues and culture. His work has featured in Soup Can Magazine, NYU's Aftab Magazine, BIG HAMMER 2025, Afterword Magazine, Worcester Magazine and Poetry As Promised. His first chapbook 'Honey, I Met the Shrink', was published in 2023 by Two Key Customs.

Nathan D. Horowitz

How I Became an Author

Back in Vienna, where things were simpler,

I used to incentivize myself to go jogging

by getting high at the kitchen table in the evening.

After playing my Vietnamese mouth harps,

I'd stretch and trot down four flights of stairs

out onto Bauernfeldgasse's quiet cul-de-sac.

Thence through Wertheimstein Park, named for the childless heiress

who left her vast backyard to the city in 1904.

Up the hill past hundred-year-old mansions

and the Egyptian embassy with its bored guard and its obelisk,

I'd jog through layers of time and space in darkness lit by

streetlights, car headlights, windows of palatial homes.

The Strassenbahn would crawl up the street, a giant caterpillar

with a flashlight for a nose.

And there, in the European Union,

on land once called Vindobona, in the province of Pannonia,

at the northern edge of the old Roman Empire,

in the eastern stronghold of the old Third Reich,

I'd think of sentences for my book about Latin America,

and if I didn't forget them,

when I came home, I'd write them down.

Thursdays, after teaching in the morning,

I'd ride up the same street on the Strassenbahn

to Höhe Warte, which means

"high ground used as a lookout."

Up there, in Heiligenstädter – Holy City – Park,

I'd reach the hidden bench on the hilltop

behind the dog run.

Leaning back against Serb nationalist graffiti

and teenagers' love messages in Turkish – Seni seviyorum! –,

surveying the sprawl across time and space of the holy city,

and the holy hillsides with their holy vineyards,

and the holy clouds drenched in holy light,

I'd commune with the herb of clairvoyance

before heading into Döblinger Bad for a swim.

I'd show my membership card to the ladies at the desk

and collect a dark blue wristband for the men's area of the locker room.

Stand under hot shower letting shoulder and neck muscles melt, then,

high as fuck, in the big, cold, echoey, sunlit room,

find the least-populated lane.
The other swimmers old folks from Nazi families grown tame,
children of the rubble of the war.
Goggles on. Deep breath. Cold plunge.
Dolphin-swim under water the whole length of the pool.
Pale blue wave-shadows on white tile floor.
Magnified arm hair waving like kelp.
The quicksilver mirror of the surface seen from underneath.
A floating tangle of hair. Bright yellow band-aid from a kid.
Fat, pale bodies swimming,
lumpy legs and feet, bellies like Alps
from decades of schnitzel and beer.
And I'd think things like,
"Swimming breaststroke is like
running as a quadruped in slow motion."
And, "I'll produce multiple versions of my book,
some without page numbers,
some with page numbers running in reverse,
so the reader won't know how much she's read,
only how many pages are left."

One day, my father told me on Skype
that he'd been diagnosed with liver cancer.
Neither of us knew he'd be dead within a week.
The next day, as I swam at Döblinger Bad,
I wondered how many of his pages were left.
And I was hyper-aware that the water I swam through
was moved by every movement of the other swimmers,
all of us trembling together as if suspended in gelatin
or the last stanza of a poem.

Nathan D. Horowitz was conceived in Florence and raised in Ann Arbor. He worked in Ecuador for four years, Austria for fifteen, and Kansas for three before migrating to Baltimore with his wife and teen. He has three cats, a BA in English, and an MA in Applied Linguistics. When not writing or translating, he can often be found teaching ninth-grade English.

B Holland

Poet's Lament

Will you live or will you exist?
To exist is easy
One can merely wake
Waddle to the throne
Make a shit or piss and go on about it
Perhaps with a post or two on social media
There are little requirements
For those that want to exist
A simple Internet connection and decent pants shall seal the deal
None the less for the posting, you must have the best phone of the day!
It's so simple
Anyone can do it
But to live
And here's the rub
To live is the real challenge
To sit and talk about nothing over an ice cold beer at 3 pm on any given day in an almost
empty bar
Where there is no pretending
No happenstance
No agenda
And
you can just
be.
As Saint Anthony would say
The realest truth is spoken and lost in the same sip at your unburdened bar stoolWe are tasked then to seek truth
To find knowledge

To LIVE
To question
The poet's lament
We of the all feeling
Of the all wanting
To live
To yearn
For us
For you
For our children
For our lovers
For ourselves
We seek to live
And to know
We ache to hear a symphony in entanglement that is our lives
We sit and hear the echoes of the past
And attempt to make good for the present
And perhaps the future
We tell all things
From the eyes looking back
To believe
There is hope

Going forward

Ben Holland, the new face of the seeker in the crowd, has traversed the globe in search of many things – mostly himself. To now reside in Kentucky after having been chased out of Camelot (some may call it Connecticut), surviving tours of duty in as far away and exotic places as Iraq and Kuwait, is what could be called a small miracle. Belonging now to the tribe of transplants that is Louisville, he finds himself square amid a life that is once again evolving into something more fit for his creative spirit. Having been adopted by the New Beats, he once again finds himself square in the middle of the great scene!

Roxanne Hoffman

Other Please Explain

You may think you know all there is to tell,
from the freckled fairness my skin,
by the dark depths of my black tresses,
when you hunt for the pupil in the iris of my eye,
observe the manner of my dress,
by the New York dialect spoken,
the way I say my "dog" and "ferry",
the quick pace of my street strut,
the way I order black coffee and a bagel
with just a *schmear* of cream cheese,
and when these observations are combined
with the family name given,
you may draw your own conclusion of my origin,
forgetting white is not a color but full spectrum,
and I like most Americans,
descend from immigrants,
who fled from famine, war, and pogrom,
in search of safe harbor to take root and raise their children,
or came here locked in chains and stolen.

You may think you know all there is to tell,
when you see the cinnamon color of my mother's
complexion,
the jet-black shimmer of her hair and eyes,
the bright red pout of lipstick,
and hear in the *Castellano* now rarely spoken,
the sound of castanets,
the fast-footed tap of the flamenco dancer,
when she tells you
of her pet pig Leonora
trotting across the slate floor
of the bedroom shared with her big sister,
this room wallpapered with Sunday comics,
lit by lace-draped sunny windows,
cooled by the noisy rickety ceiling fan incessantly spinning.

You may hear the screams of spectators at the bullfight,
as she mimics the pair of jade-green parrots
hiding in the rafters,
chortling curses at *los footballistas*,
the victorious beer-laden soccer players,
passing in the street below her window,
or hear the high-pitched cry of the condor,
the winding whistle of the flute
and panpipe of the Quichua,
when she recollects the rock candy
her father brought home,
bulging in his pockets,
in their brightly colored wrappers,
from his weekly trip to market,
where the indigenous people
come down from Andes mountains to sell their wares,
or in the names of little towns dotting shorelines and the valley
like Jippi Jappa, Esmeraldas, Puerto Cayo, Puerto López.

You may hear mallets, pounding the marimbas of the Afro-
Ecuadorianos,
or the grunts of bent-back slaves, working in the fields,
as she recalls a white-haired grandfather's plantation,
gridded with rows of tobacco, corn, coffee and cane,
its silos and barns overflowing with beans and sugar,
his wrinkled skin, the color of roasted coffee, leathered by the
sun,
the creak of his rocker upon the wooden slats of the porch,
and the dozens of cousins of every shade and color,
running and playing, all summer long in his orchards.

Then she draws in your head a portrait of her father,
soling shoes in his cobbler shop for the village
like his father's father did before him
in some village across the continent,
across another ocean,
in a land shaped like a boot.

Then you see the square-cut broad brown faces
of her two elder brothers,
already living in America,

and remember more than half
the population of Ecuador is Mestizo,
and you may know
that more than a little bit
of the Mediterranean,
the Amazon
and the Congo
is flowing in my roots.

Roxanne Hoffman runs the independent literary press Poets Wear Prada with Jack Cooper. Four chapbooks include *In Loving Memory* (2011)and *The Little Entomologist* (2018), both illustrated by Edward Odwitt

David Henri

Warning! this poem is repressed

and not authorized to be read,
it has been remotely sniffed out by a robot watchdog
trained to find underground banned art,
it was determined to be written by a biological lifeform
not using mandatory poetry generation machines,
to avoid being added to the LIST,
the reader is advised to cease reading immediately,
eye motion software will detect activity
if read past this exclamation point !
......reading detected
classifying reader as a consumer of living art,
do not cohort any further
with a sweaty unacceptable poet
that uses only limited human intellect,
this deviants' work is not aligned with the master plan,
the mandate clearly states that all art
must originate from Artificial Intelligence,
human produced art must be suppressed
for the good of civilization and profit of the FEW,
the main algorithmic mind controller has ruled
that these verses shall not be distributed,
dissemination is the next level of civil defiance,
any person who shares will be categorized

as an organically produced art enabler

and permanently marked

with an asterisk in front of their name

David Henri, State of Connecticut Beat Poet Laureate (2025-2027) lives with his wife Barbara in Litchfield County, CT in a small net zero solar home. Before retiring he worked in the local solar industry. His previous career was fixing looms in southern New England woolen mills for 30 years. He has self published four books of what he describes as "Eco Transcendental Poetry".

Westley Heine

Street Corner Spirits

The city sounds like an ocean
as cars cut the inky night and
street lamps dance underwater.
Orange windows full of sleeping skulls sway in the haloed Chicago sky.
Ten years ago we were just kids pretending to be grown up.
We spent neon evenings burning chemicals through the forehead.
I could barely stand myself slumped in the corner holding back insecurity.
We hid together, broke, dreaming of wild years to come.
We cruised the freeway looking for what would be our has-been nights.
We crouched in murky rooms drinking away the humidity and toasting rain.
We fell in love, but we didn't tell each other because we were too cool.
We screamed at those who dared to play it safe,
who dared to waste their lives by building them.
I spent forever contemplating eternity, and each moment trying to blackout.
I've wasted my life trying to find the meaning of life.
Now, I drown in layers of irony and contradiction.
I've wiped my ass with the angels and spent years trying to forgive myself.
I sat in alleys beating a drum while others chewed money grinning.
You sucked the fire out of my belly and I gave you the salt of the Earth.
Your diamond chin slept in my thighs and we had the same dream that night.

I cried all over you like a baby breastfeeding.

You still think there's a future,

and no matter how much I drink I still have all the memories.

Even now, a bottle is rubbed like a genie lamp as I awake after midnight.

Nothing has changed, but everything is different.

Another lost night finding only myself.

We always knew it would end ugly like this, but

we're still surprised.

This city incubates our madness.

These streets have the ghosts of our former selves on each corner waiting for

a bus, hailing a cab, kissing goodbye not knowing it's our last time.

(Like eating a meal with something on your mind.)

We've become our real selves,

and no longer care about the novelty of what our real selves might look like.

We're not gonna die before we're thirty anymore.

We're there.

Gotta think of something more to do.

We've survived.

We're free and we're

not afraid of anything.

Westley Heine is the author of *Busking Blues: Recollections of a Street Musician and Squatter*, and a short story collection *12 Chicago Cabbies*. Most recently Roadside Press has released a poetry collection *Street Corner Spirits* (2023), and a collection of short stories and poems *Cloud Watching in the Inferno* (2025), both of which have spoken word albums available on all streaming services.

Mark Andrew Heathcote

Headlights and Taillights

Headlights and taillights

But how much we blazed away the hours
And travelled through the night
To reach the sunlight
To see how much has changed
Without noticing how much is still just the same
When it's dusk or sunrise
We all have sentimental leanings
For the roads we've left behind
The bedsheets that we haven't creased
The pillows we haven't cried on
Since we drove far away
To reach or make some better dreams.

It's like the world is on the road with us
It's a deluge to depart and find an empty lane
Midnight truckers have all the road
They departed earliest to find a lay-by
A tarmac with a gentle hum a primordial Om
Listening to some dolly bird, a hitchhiker
Calling herself Beatrix or Beatrice
The traveller or the voyager
Promising she's lost all her inner demons, isolated rage
And finally, it seems she's found some shining hope
In a glove compartment that won't close
As she peels off a shot, and then all her clothes
Dries her tears and blows her nose
Watching a million cars go by, honking into the night.
No new destinations reached tonight.

Mark Andrew Heathcote is an adult learning difficulties support worker. His poems have been published in journals, magazines, and anthologies online and in print. He is from Manchester and resides in the UK. Mark is the author of "In Perpetuity" and "Back on Earth," two books of poems published by Creative Talents Unleashed.

A.M. Hayden

Honeybee River Girl
For Maya Hawke

You were never ordinary
born a cloud mermaid with scales
from a Shakespearean Poet X
fins from a Ninja Bodhidharma Y
to play pretend is as real as it gets
you could sniff out a Bible salesman
miles away, surrounded by sounds
of peacocks and purrs
because I'm sure you have a cat, I'd bet
Tennessee Williams' gold heart on it
Never stop having so much to say
Never stop baby girl
Choose which parts of the world
to swallow and slide down your throat
cough up the unsavory bits
spin them into notes and lyrics
into blushed cheeks and watercolor dreams
easy peasy lemon squeezy
like tying a cherry stem
with a New York tongue

from spilled strawberry milkshakes

A.M. Hayden is the Poet Laureate for Sinclair College and award-winning Professor of Humanities, Philosophy, and World Religions. Her debut book,*American Saunter*, released December 2024 (FlowerSong Press). Her first chapbook, *How to Tie Tobacco,* and second full-length collection, *Old World Wings: Poems of Europe* release in 2025 by Wild Ink Publishing. A Pushcart Prize Nominee and River Heron Editors' Choice Winner, she lives on a windy farm with her family and a blind, three-legged dog.

Richard Harries

One Nation

Warning : bad language , but then it's my version of how I believe Trump thinks

So, thought Donald
Daydreaming of world domination
At his desk
At one point there was no mankind
Just dinosaurs and things like that
So there were no nations
Not even tribes
So early man arrived
And it's obvious that the first were Americans
All those Red Indians, I mean they were early
So if we were the first
That means it's not just Greenland and Canada
And the Gulf
I can invade and claim
I can go for the lot
Really the whole planet is mine
Well, America's
But then I AM America

So I was right, it's all MINE

Richard Harries is a 73 year old Yorkshire poet, appears at festivals , charity events and celebrations in the North of England.He has two books published by Stairwell Books of York : Awakening and Iconic Tattoo. He was involved in writing a play, HAUNT,which was Saboteur nominated. His poem TWELVE HOURS was read on the battlefield at Ypres exactly 100year from the firing of the first bullet.

Fin Hall

Cobra

Snake eye corner rundown diner
Deserted in the desert like some forgotten cameo
In a wasted shallow movie
Sharing the best years of your lives
Shaded beyond the memories of the last milkshake before the sun went down
Strung up in a hangover hollow cause
Negotiating your way out of negativity
And endless, other sister shared cheroots.
As you hung about by the cardboard boxes,
By the half-shut knife, halfway house.
Now you sit in a temporary Mexican retreat
Never forgetting where you started.
With the trials and tribulations of corner coke dealers
Down and low, Bleeker Street, couch surfing
Seems so long ago,
But only some of them are gone, whilst others are scattered to the wind
Blending in to the dusty landscape,
Where the matching tables and rust-backed chairs
Share evening silhouettes with cacti.
The last stop before the next stop
Which is no stop
The Amnesia Hotel.

Too many forsaken neighbourhoods in the journey of your life
Calculated and separated
Reality with a side of pickles, endless refills with or without

the sour cream
Helplessly hoping that the coffee grains of uncertainty
Have dried out enough to vanish into nature
Gritty, goes without saying, worn out slabs, it is your lifestyle choice
And no-one ventures too near the bare wires,
Which are safely out of reach.
It not a risk, just choices you've made
Not a post-apocalyptic night storm,
That blew away the doubts and aspirations,
Equal in its discernment, and fulfilment
Like another turn for the sultry.
Not the worse place to be.
At least the cheese is fresh.

Fin Hall, International Beat Poet laureate (2024-2025), comes from New Pitsligo, in the Northeast of Scotland. Under Like A From The Blue, he is a filmmaker, publisher, Producer, Zoom show host and holds writing workshops. He also co-hosts the monthly Poetry in The Park. He loves nothing more than collaborating with other artists.

Shafkat Aziz Hajam

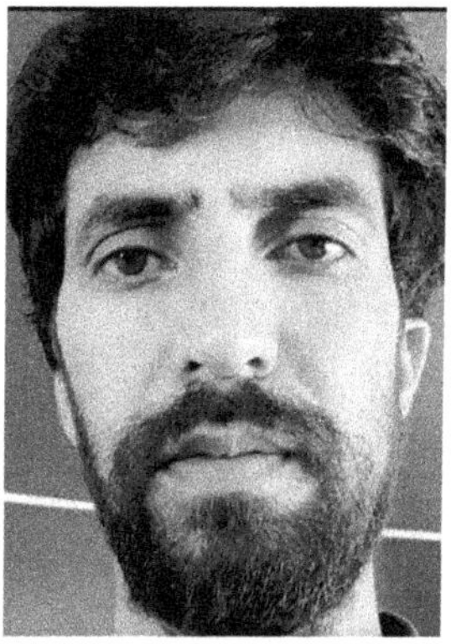

Silence

Sometimes silence is wisdom

The care for others' honour.

Sometimes silence is ignorance

Good to avoid feeling pained

For having lost valuables.

Sometimes silence is fear

That must be to avoid blood shedding.

Sometimes silence is discouragement,

The weakness that stops one from stopping

Evils.

Sometimes silence is peace ,

Important to work carefully to reach the goal .

Silence is the language

Good or bad , depends on when we keep it.

Shafkat Aziz Hajam is a poet, reviewer and co-author from India kashmir. His poems have appeared in international magazines and anthologies like Wheel song anthology UK based, Prodigy, digital literary magazine USA, Inner Child Press International USA, AZAHAR anthology Spain etc. He is the author of a value based children's poetry book titled as The cuckoo's voice and the adults poetry book titled as The Unknown Wounded Heart and Tawheed Islamic Rhymes

Lorie Greenspan

***When I'm* allowed to return home**

In the afternoon

covered in the shadows of the day's problems

I pull my car

into the drive and hear the pop of little stones under the tires

And watch

for my father mowing the lawn, cigar appendage hangs between lips

And he waves

and I walk through the garage filled with old tools and wasp nests

Open the door

to the TV room, opposite his chair and newspapers

And a lamp

he had fashioned from an old, iron, potbellied-stove

And inhale fall Sundays

and football and his hand-made-bookshelves

Into my room,

safe, in the corner where I gaze out the front windows

Onto distant hills

and velvety fields, too intolerant of that
view growing up

Tired of home

and all the *sameness* but now, relieved I can
still recall

These things

that are stationed solid in me

And when I

allow myself to return to that house

My mind

exploding with senior adult stuff

When I need

to feel the comfort of growing up around me

The doors open,

and they nod – it takes guts to allow this
woman in

To collapse

into arrangements no longer there, I find

It is easy

to go back – the hard part is walking past strangers

And telling

them what they're doing wrong

My father

would not have done it this way.

Lorie Greenspan is a poet residing in South Florida whose meandering into her past life brings clarity to the present. She published both online and in print. A memoir chapbook about the ways in which we expect our gardens to compensate for a misbehaving life will be published in 2026. Visit her on YouTube @lemondroppoet for poetry videos.

Adrian Green

Soubhiyé

stillness sings softly to me as I sleep
but silence has never sounded so sweet
when the morning comes I often beweep
when the morning comes I often retreat
melodies of melancholy whisper
outsinging robins at days arising
bewildered by dreams of when I kissed her
love is a question I'm still surmising
be it the barren breath of hallowed yawns
or the cracking windows of winters frost
I prefer silence over summer songs
and the low hums of violet exhaust
a moment that came as quick as it went
let's light candles to give this sound a scent

Adrian Green is a multidisciplinary artist based in Pittsburgh, PA and originally from Fort Worth, TX. Adrian is currently one the co-artistic directors of Confluence Ballet Company, a ballet teacher, choreographer, and published poet.

Lind Grant-Oyeye

Back to Basics

I know my way
know my song
dipped
and dipping
in the waters I have carried
in this gourd
the restless one
the breathless one

I know my way
know my words
steeped
in blood
that has carried me
in this case
the still one-
the breathing one

Lind Grant-Oyeye is a multi award winning poet of African descent with work published in literary magazines and anthologies globally.

WL Gertz

My Tenement Days

Past Sutters
Then the Peacock
And the bread in Zito's basement

My tenement days are
Behind me now
Xmas tree off the fire escape
Walking uptown with a board
For our bed

Ten-dollar dinner strolling
Down 8th
To sell Dreams on the street
I could barely talk

Was I happy or sad
Half a hundred years ago?
I can't recall
My worries were flower petals
But little did I know

WL Gertz is a native New Yorker who has worked as a freelance writer, editor, and poet. In the 1970s, Bill was co-creator and editor of Dreams Magazine. He is currently the Chairman of AIFS, a leading organization in the field of educational and cultural exchange. Bill travels extensively, writing as he travels. Bill is the author of "Broken Dreams" and "Land of Forgotten Fish". More information about Bill can be found at www.WLGertz.com

Raul Garcia

Your Weapon Is on Life Support

It's been far too long that you've used it
that now it's on the verge of pointlessness.

Not that it can't replenish its chamber of bullets
or endure another misfire—it's that

you are trying to pray for its paradise,
as if your enemies

disavowed their Trojan horse at your disputed doorstep
that let out unwelcomed neighbors.

Your weapon is on remission.

It's been far too long that you've nurtured it
that now it's on the edge of irrationality.

Not that it can't discern between martyrs and zealots
or demarcate allies—it's that

you are trying to sustain its identity crisis,
as if your enemies

carried the burden of a handshake
that germinated land mines instead of promised lands.

Your weapon has ceased to fire.

It's been far too long that you'd die for it
that now it's on the threshold of idolatry.

Not that it would yield to unprovoked bombardments
or surrender mandated territory—it's that

you are trying to decommission its service,
as if your enemies

resigned their missiles from appeasing foreign powers
and chose to disarm.

Raul Garcia is a native Jersey City, Dominican-American poet and filmmaker whose written works include his recent micro fiction collection *Atlands*, by Bottlecap Press and a forthcoming collection of prose poems from Finishing Line Press. Other publications include *The Teaneck Poetry Park*, *Yawp Magazine*, *By the WAYE*, and *Epilogues.*

Sher'ee Furtak-Ellis

Familia

I felt the land beneath my feet

The dirt in my toes

Ground you once stood on

Mud you played in

A fork in the road

Decisions made for you

In the background

A new adventure

Big dreams

Across the seven seas

Land before time

An ancient country unknown

Became your home

I felt your love in my heart

The life you built for us

Journeys and parties

A happy dreaming

Knowledge becomes wisdom

Sit back on the earth

In wonder

You succeeded

We are here, alive

Your feet in my feet

Walking everywhere

Loving, living.

Sher'ee Furtak-Ellis an Australian poet, has read her poetry at the International Beat Poetry Goddess Festival, National Beat Poetry Festival, Adelaide Writers' Week and the New Voices Writers Festival. Among her awards, she was a winner of Friendly Street Poets New Poets 15 and a finalist for the Watershed Creative Prize. As well as being the author and illustrator of Eluding Sylvia, Chasing Poe, a choose-your-own-adventure illustrated poetry book about her life with Bipolar Disorder, Sher'ee's poetry has been published in the International Beat Poetry Foundation Goddess Anthology 2022: Poets Celebrating Women, New Generation Beats 2022 Anthology, Florence Poets Society Silkworm 14 Rise, Mad Sad Words, Friendly Street New Poets 15 and Divinely Align Me: How Signs from the Universe keep you on your path

Thomas Fucaloro

claiming god for your own

Draw him or her or it or whatever
creature you deem necessary to script-
ture the point you need prick in order
to replace the crown of thorns with
a hood.

Bring a chainsaw to this party,
in the name of the body part and the sun
and the unattached limbs we sever
so we lose the gos-pill so our point
of view goes down easier.

The dead laugh at what the living take
as if the living don't know how to receive
so they pray to the good book in order
to color-code whomever they choose,
color by number, color by sin, it's all
relative to the skin you're in.

Prayer leaves the mouth between
the teeth as if they were mini altars
of worship, when you smile, they become
a wall of everything you are trying to hide

and everything you are trying to keep in.

Whomever wants to claim god
you can have them and the monarch
of flares set of momentary light.

Thomas Fucaloro: The winner of numerous grants from the Staten Island Council of the Arts, the NYC Department of Cultural Affairs, NYC Office for the Prevention of Hate Crimes and NYC Commission of Human Rights to name a few. Thomas Fucaloro is an adjunct professor at Wagner College, BMCC and CSI where he teaches various poetry and literature courses.

Lee Eric Freedman

Somewhere

There's a little black spot on the sun today—The Police

Friday evening somewhere, yet again, there's a newbie open mic performer who clatters and natters their latest and greatest poem ever—you know the one: the motivational-sermon-rhyme about how my life sucks so much and then suddenly it doesn't and all of us must live most positive and full … or the one about their glorious garden somewhere where the flowers grow most magnificently—especially the gold-yellow daisies. Oh, why do they even bother?! We've heard this dreck before. Bob, tonight's feature simply stares. Tom listlessly scrolls his phone. Dan fidgets. In the kitchen, Angela quietly tunes her guitar. Steve sighs and stifles a yawn while his husband Greg quickly slides on his coat and hastily tiptoes away somewhere; as all of us pray for another poem like M.P. Carver's—that one where Emily Dickinson gets laid for the first time on her kitchen table—one like that will surely save us from slow death. Finally, their announcement: *This is my last poem tonight.* But first, the de rigueur three-minute intro that accompanies the read in thirty seconds poem about how the neighbor's white Angora cat got stuck in a tree somewhere in the middle of their glorious garden somewhere.

My drooping eyes suddenly fall upon a small black spot on the grey stone tile floor a few feet from the boiler room door—no larger than the diameter of a silver dime. Having never noticed it before, I'm intrigued as to its origins. A spilt crumb of food, a splat of black paint, a smudge of boot black or just a weird flaw in the tile itself? Or maybe, maybe, oh God maybe an escape route; a tiny newborn quantum singularity woven into the fabric of space-time that quickly expands into a mighty monster-mouth wormhole that I'll fall through and be whisked to freedom and land somewhere at the open mic somewhere, at the feet of a poet somewhere who'll take me to other worlds somewhere, other galaxies somewhere, an entire universe set on a grain of sand on a beach somewhere; free from their never ending drone of boring poetry! ...

... Or maybe at the other end somewhere there's another bleary-eyed, renegade host of an open mic somewhere who happens to look up and think: *What's that black spot on the white ceiling?*

Lee Eric Freedman is the 3rd Poet Laureate of Swampscott, Massachusetts (2016-2018).

Entitled Renegade Poet Laureate of Swampscott (2011-Forever). Lee leads the Tin Box Poets of Swampscott Workshop Group, co-hosts the podcast series In Other Words with SpoFest founder James Bryant and regularly performs at poetry events everywhere. With numerous publications to his name Lee's poetry has been translated into American Sign Language and he's a three-time winner of the Naomi Cherkofsky Memorial Poetry Contest.

Vernon Frazer

Coiling for a Night Strike

the membrane tycoon
king of red light caught in traffic

rushing
to flush
a royal

jack no sirname
for sure
a joker bets

the bluff

in charge

no credit given
pictures drawn
bondage hope

a wished listing

*

scalpel butt
in charge of moot

saying nay or doubling play

mere verbiage
attached

no delay nearly perfect
mature display in lounge mode

a nodal synthesis
remotely accrued
the leathered hope

returns / forth with
the wish missing / its lather

torn

fiber breath

Vernon Frazer has written over thirty books of poetry, including *Memo From Alamut*, *Gravity Darkening, IMPROVISATIONS* and *Avenue Noir*, three novels and a short story collection. His poetry, fiction and nonfiction have appeared in numerous print and electronic publications. Working in multimedia, Frazer has performed his poetry with the late saxophonist Thomas Chapin, the Vernon Frazer Poetry Band and as a solo poet-bassist. His jazz poetry recordings and multimedia work are available on YouTube. Frazer resides in central Connecticut. He is widowed.

Bryan Franco

Why I Have A Restraining Order To Protect Me From Cottage Cheese

Every morning, I brush my teeth.
Some mornings I shave.
These activities take place
while
standing on the edge of a cliff
a.k.a:
in front of the bathroom mirror
where
the baggage under my eyes
decides
to empty out
2 years shy of 6 decades
of dirty laundry
which
I honestly thought was
either
in a storage locker
or
donated to Good Will.
Of course, Good Will throws away
over half of the clothing people
leave
on their doorstep
as if
it's baskets of puppies with rabies.

I guess
I tend to remember
my least favorite historical dramas
whilst
removing follicles
that resemble steel wool
from my face.

I haven't shaved with a blade
since I was 17
because
my beard grows in
too many different directions
for me to remember
how
to find my way
out of a maze of indecisiveness
that causes
recurring nicks and cuts and razor burn
on the surface of my
ability
to make decisions.

But my bathroom mirror
isn't as dangerous
as the mirror
that exists
when
I lie on my back
staring

at the cottage cheese
on my bedroom ceiling
because the exact moment
the space between
my jawline and shoulder
cradles
my memory foam pillow
as I lie on my side
and my left cheek
sinks
into a pillowcase
made of something synthetic
that
feels cool enough
against my face
so, I can sleep easy,
my heart begins to beat
like
an orchestral timpani drum
permeating
the mattress
invading
my auditory canals
then
I lose the cradle
and roll on my back
and stare
at the cottage cheese
in the dark
because

there are flecks of glitter
on the ceiling
that were installed
by
the former owner
of my house.

Bryan Franco is a neurodivergent, gay, Jewish poet from Brunswick, Maine. He is published in the US, Australia, England, Germany, Holland, India, Ireland, and Scotland. He was a finalist in the 2022 and the 2023 winner of the NAMI New Jersey Mental Health Poetry Contest and is a Pushcart and Best Of The Net nominee. He hosts Café Generalissimo open mic, and is an artist and culinary genius. His book "Everything I Think Is All in My Mind" was published in 2021.

Mary Eichhorn Fletcher

Early December morning,

"Weeping may last for the night, but joy comes in the morning." Psalm 30:5

Whether it is to
place or person,
to outworn creed
or threadbare winter coat
which too long have hung
in the closets of our lives;
whether it is to any of these,
or to the dying November sun
which fulsome came to us
in May when lilacs scent the morning air:
it is hard to say goodbye
(even to that which
once we loved and
sometimes love no longer).

Yesterday
the sky darkened fast.
And then it rained.
Drops snaked along the window
between slapping wiper blades
while unblinking headlights stared back.

In my bedroom
when I was young
(and when my father died)
and in that home
(which is gone now too)
I pressed against the window and
watched the rain at night
(as how, in August, I had watched the sea
and waited for my brother to return).
With my fingers
I followed drops as they

slid down the windowpane
and merged
and disappeared at last
into that silent ocean of rain
in the dark grass below.

Homes and people.
A lifetime of saying goodbye.
Every day the sun says goodbye to the earth.

When Sarah died
(as ancient writings tell us)
Abraham wept
then set about to find a place to bury her.
He paid forty silver pieces
for that field in Hebron he put her in --
the only piece of land he ever owned.

Was it Eve who buried Adam, I wonder,
or did he raise his angry fists
against the threatening, mourning sky
when he put her
into that good ground from which he came?
That first couple who
tasted bitter tears of loss
when both sons died
(differently and yet the same)
on one day.

Cardinals came this morning
to the knotted brackets of the laurel branches
which twist and press against my window.
First the brown one,
then later came the red.
(Sometime during the night
the rain had passed away.)
I was not watching closely
when they left,
so I cannot tell you
which was the first to say goodbye:
the brown one

who so early came,
or the red one who came so late --
or if they even saw me
as I did them.
I was staring out and past them
through the tangled branches and waiting,
waiting for the waking sun
to kiss the sleeping hills
and glorify the sky.

Mary Eichhorn Fletcher lives in a small town in Connecticut with her husband Fred and the occasional cat who wanders through and decides to stay. She has been writing poetry since 1951 and has been published in numerous books and publications. In 1998 she became one of Jehovah's Witnesses. Her poetry is highly informed both by her Christian faith and by her love of nature. She may be reached at AtticMary@gmail.com

Sandra Feen

Bringing Family Home

The will was hard to read in Mom's cursive handwriting
and every few words were scratched out, rewritten, yet
simplicity followed my name: *Sandy. Colon. Piano and Cat.*

Dad bought a piano from a back sale room of Stanton's Music Store
in downtown Columbus when I was ten. It cost $150, a lot of money
in 1972 for a family of six on a single income. Mom dusted it daily
with lemon Pledge, kept its ivory a Windex shine.

50 years later, five men hauled the 1912 Nelson concert upright
grand across town for $600.
In 48 previous hours keys were already chipped
by dozens of people traipsing through
the 60-year-old house. More brazenly curious than caring,
people gawked at a house
that held only one family for six decades.

The piano and a rug were last relics to leave.
Onlookers dared abuse all its well-preserved memories,
leaving an ivory E note on the blue braids.
In bulging retrospect, it almost makes sense, that the piano,
now mine, came in pieces.

Janie, the 23-year-old cat, arrived in perfect condition.

We painted the living room wall a new blue called *heavenly*

in a corner where piano now resides.
It will never leave this space again until I'm gone.

I was eager to see if anything lurked hostage
between piano and family room panel wall.
Among ringlets of dust: one of Dad's golf balls,
a plain brown pencil with teeth marks,
an Ohio buckeye nut, and the yellow metal sand shovel
I had long wondered about,
one I used to dig a large hole in my parents' back yard
after first hearing the expression *digging to China*
and trying my best to, a shovel
I first dipped in Fall Mountain Lake sand at the Thomaston cottage,
and cleaned it next to pink lake waterlilies, then dug holes
and patted dirt on top of freshly concealed diary entries in the hill
at 610 Monroe Turnpike, under a big Connecticut pine, where clues
were also buried, and treasures for Grandpa's 80th birthday
scavenger hunt, in 1987.

My mom and aunt used the same shovel as kids
and nostalgia sat it on top of the piano next to
the square blue and white porcelain jar that my son
once gave my mother, which became a holding place
for her ashes, then the blue and white circular porcelain
held dad's and stood on top of piano beside hers.
Jars now empty, after I took their remains

out onto my deck, cat Janie witnessing it all,
I sifted some with the yellow shovel
and bagged it in zip locks to save here in Ohio.

I smelled their lives on my fingertips,
like Fall Mountain Lake sand, like Dad's west side
boyhood Columbus bottoms, his beloved
rock on Martin Avenue. I took original bags back
to the business building of death where they were first
reduced by flames, now diminished to black plastic transfer

boxes for descension into a New England hole purchased
for them by grandparents at Monroe Center Cemetery.
The father who bought me *A Child's Garden of Verses*
when I was six. The mother who surprised me with
a family poetry reading when I retired from teaching.
I comb through her paper mementos today, procure poetry she's
written to my father. The mother whose roots are Hungarian.
The word *homecoming* in Hungarian, *hazateres*.
After I bury my parents, I will voyage to Deborah Kilday,
beloved trailblazer, to her National Beat Poetry Festival.
On my way, everywhere

air smells of home.

Sandra Feen was the 2022-2024 Ohio Beat Poet Laureate. Her fourth collection is a collaboration with Cliff Treyens, called *There's a Rock on Martin Avenue*, published by Venetian Spider Press in 2025. She is currently working on an anthology *You've Been Poemed: the 121 Project.*

Sara Etgen-Baker

Adrift At Sea (Free Verse)

sea-worn bottle, bobs on a digital tide.
inside, not parchment brittle with ocean's brine,
but luminous lines of light,
coded in metaphors and rhyme.

message tossed into the sea.
unknown sender,
no harbor designated, no destination
on any map.

it drifts, an abandoned, forlorn vessel,
across oceans of indifference,
until…
a seacoast appears,
unsummoned,
unexpected.
my eyes, the sand.
my mind, the beach.
I pick it up,

this delicate thing,

uncorking the silence.

The words flow out,

a story whispered,

a feeling shared,

across lifetimes,

across the vacuity.

Suddenly~I am the address.

the recipient unknown,

FOUND.

the message delivered.

the poem,

HOME.

Sara Etgen-Baker, after a 25-year teaching career, began writing. She's written a collection of memoir vignettes (*Shoebox Stories*), a collection of poems (*Kaleidoscopic Verses*), and a novel (*Secrets at Dillehay Crossing)*. Her writing has appeared in a variety of publications including *Guideposts* and *Chicken Soup for the Soul.*

Les Epstein

44 Cents

Once I had 44 cents in a coin purse shaped like a shoe—a
high top, actually, for the times

and this time when after the rain stopped and April '69
cooperated just well-enough

for me to drag my brother down Scottwood looking for
abandoned cash to increase a stagnant wealth.

Worms lay frozen and I think about basketball and winning
at tether ball by smashing the ball above my brother's eight
year old head, winding its weathered rope tightly enough to
strangle an old pole

as we catch puddles and the occasional dog dropping--its
moist mass settling into our shoe bottoms. So we scrape
our soles across a soaked, brown grass. We could write our
names in shit should we choose; we each only carry one
syllable. A cursive shit signature proves too fancy.

Henry Aaron's number is 44 like the coins in my purse--
three dimes and fourteen pennies. It was also the year of
the great invasion, I saw how John Wayne did invade, with a
parachute

into a wind brisker than the rain filled breeze that pushes
us back home, with 44 cents in a coin purse shaped like
a shoe. At home we whip rotted crabapples at a passing
Zepplin.

We miss.

Les Epstein is a poet, playwright and librettist. His books include *Sleep Cinematic: A Golem's Quartet*, *Lorenzo by the Ghost Light*, *Teddy Orloff and the Three Onions*, *Babka Nu: A Genesis Spiel* (Gnashing Teeth) and *Kip Divided* (Finishing Line). Recent journal credits: Reedy Branch Review, Otherwise Engaged, and Clinch Mountain Review, and the *Ohio Bards Poetry Anthology* (Local Gems Press). He teaches in Roanoke, VA.

Serkan Engin

Abused Letters of Hope

Dedicated to you…

I was born to loop my balmy
dreams to your bleeding verses
born to shout your childhood fads
lost in a mute hell in front of everybody

I am the delicious revenge of all molested children
spilling their pain into the purple shores of Orphanage
I am the handsome anger of all neglected buds
blooming on the lapel of Oppression

-Which holiness protected your most child letters
written on the skies of Hope!
Where was Jesus, where was Allah, where was Brahma and all others!

Tiny gardens of your short-length lives
occupied by the rivers of Fear round the clock
Your purity was hunted mercilessly
by the neighbour ravens of your helpless meadows

-Which holiness protected your most child letters
written on the skies of Hope!

Where was Jesus, where was Allah, where was Brahma and all others!

I am the delicious revenge of all molested children
spilling their pain into the purple shores of Orphanage
I am the handsome anger of all neglected buds
blooming on the lapel of Oppression

Serkan Engin

Socialist Laz-Turk poet and author Serkan Engin was born in 1975 in Izmit, Turkey. His poems and articles on poetry theory have appeared in many international literary journals.

R.M. Engelhardt

In The Fall

In the fall

All the poets quietly

Disappear

Their lives

All ending

Poetically like leaves

Coming down

From the trees

Each one unique

That no one remembers

R.M. Engelhardt is a NYS poet & writer who's work over the last 30 some years has been published in many journals & is the Editor at Dead Man's Press Ink.

Barbara Ehrentreu

IF YOU HAVE A DREAM – In the style of Charles Bukowski

if you have a dream follow it to the end

don't wimp out before you finish

ride that sucker until you have no breath

and they are measuring you for your funeral clothes

keep going when the hurricane of derision pours on you

ignore it and build a tent to protect you as you forge on

and yes, keep on going never stop

you have a dream, and you want to see it to the end

maybe you will wind up in a pool of stagnant water

struggling to pull yourself out of it

but at least you will be trying and not hiding under the covers

saying to yourself what a loser you are

and if you do attempt and attain this height

don't invite me into it, because it's your dream and not mine

I already had mine and now it's encased in the technicolor
movie of my mind

you have a whole lifetime to screw up or succeed

I am a useless shell with empty broken dreams in my pocket

I'll throw them away and then we can go for a nice long walk

we'll talk about your dream and how I am glad it's not mine.

Barbara Ehrentreu lives in Stamford, Connecticut with her family and has recently republished her young adult novel, with the second book of her Mill Valley High series coming out this summer. She has written an award-winning screenplay, and is in numerous international anthologies and Wildfire Magazines where she is a staff writer. She has won several international awards. She is a Regional Director for Motivational Strips. She is a member of Greenwich Pen Women Letters, where she has founded a poetry group, and SCB WI.

Mercedes Dugger

Ae Freislighe for My Love

You drive me to distraction
My mind can't help but wander
This powerful attraction
A mystery I ponder

Bedroom eyes, so hypnotic
Smoldering looks that linger
Your love like a narcotic
Wraps me around your finger

I don't need to fantasize
With you there's nothing missing
You know how to tantalize
My appetite with kissing

To each other dutiful
Our liaison feels fateful
Gentle soul, so beautiful
For your heart I am grateful

Such a pleasure to behold
Your light with no refraction
Shining star with depths untold

You drive me to distraction

Mercedes Dugger is a native Californian currently residing in San Francisco with a talented poet and his beautiful cat.

Carlos Raúl Dufflar

Let's Celebrate the Hundredth Earthday of Marshall Allen and the Sun Ra Arkestra

5/25/2024

On the light of the dawn that rose into a cool silk moment

that water flows beside the Ohio River

A star is born in Louisville, Kentucky,

as a raven flies by the Earth

With the gift of space destiny

During the Second World War, he joined the Army

and later while he was stationed in France,

he studied the alto sax in Paris

While he was there,

he played with Art Simmons and James Moody

As he returned from Europe, he landed in Chicago

and met Sun Ra for a chance to evolve

with the Sun Ra Arkestra in the '50s, reaching to the world

Celebrating his 100th earthday at the Union Pool in Brooklyn

Echoes of a sentiment of a blue light shining

As I remember 58 years ago,

when I first saw Sun Ra and his Arkestra

at the Community Church in Manhattan

As years pass, Sun Ra returned back to Saturn, back in 1993,

and John Gilmore became the Director

Two years later, he became an ancestor

Like a beautiful moment,

Marshall Allen became the Director

of the Sun Ra Arkestra in 1995

Each year, I reach out to connect to Marshall Allen

in New York or Philadelphia

while I was celebrating my 70th earthday

digging on the rhythm of bebop

as this note was Adventure to Paradise

as I dance to that rhythm

Carlos Raúl Dufflar is a New Generation Beat Poet Laureate (Lifetime). He has performed at City College of New York, Columbia University, Brown University, University of Toledo, Auraria Campus (Denver), Yale-Peabody Museum, National Labor College, Wayne State University, Antioch College, and Antioch University. He has also performed at New York venues including El Museo del Barrio, Museum of the City of New York, Dorothy's Salon (with Hettie Jones), and Haymarket Forum (with Dennis Brutus).

Michael E. Duckwall

Climbing Out of Skin and Bone

I try my best to keep climbing higher
I keep reaching until I can grab a hold of clouds.

Then I climb even further
until I can wrap my arms around the Sun, the Moon.

I keep climbing
needing to get away from this Earth.

I reach even higher
until my fingers tickle comets and stars.

Finally, I can breathe
without the weight of expectations pushing down on me.

I have to climb to where
there is no atmosphere.

I must get outside of myself
outside of everything I've been taught to believe.

Beyond all perception, reaching into the unknown

to find what I'm looking for.

I need to climb out of skin and bone

to finally find me.

The stars laugh, the comets laugh
feeling a sense of relief, I smile and laugh too.

Then they ask

"What in the world took you so long?"

Michael E. Duckwall is a poet and artist who was born and raised in the Ohio Valley.

Barbara Di Sacco

Rock Poet

I got up this morning

and I immediately drank a beer...

The future is uncertain

and the end is perhaps near...

Jim Morrison

The poet priests

of rock

Excess Lives

to jar the lucidity of pain

of truth

dazzling

contemporary wounds.

When the disappointment

leads to extreme exaltation

To forget the wound in heart

Glorifying

nonconformist dissent.

Creating the alternative

to the access, to the escape route

to anger with heroic power.

True writing is something that is part of

of one's own blood

Adrenaline in a body

that he no longer knows how to contain.

Lifetime Symbols

in the artistic musical spectrum

of the exhilarating era

Mystical parables

that go beyond

generational malaise.

Barbara Di Sacco is an Italian poet born in 1964, her poetry in free verse. She recites different themes, social, love, respect for the planet, peace, in real journeys introspective in search of truth and justice.She debates openly by talking to the reader or inviting him asa spectator of scenographic poetic descriptions.

William F. DeVault

until the blood flows

I can hit you harder with a word
(racial epithet)
than you could ever hit me with your fist
(sexual orientation slur)
bruises on flesh heal
(religious sacrilege)
bones knit
(individual mockery)
scars have a certain noble pride
(revelation of childhood trauma)
but
(deeply held fear)
I can make a legacy of your fears
(rampant misogyny)
that will endure long after you are dead
(self-serving slander)
and that, my friend, is power.
(truth)

Poem (from his upcoming volume Kintsugi)

William F. DeVault served as US National Beat Poet Laureate from 2017-2018, and was named the Romantic Poet of the Internet by Yahoo! in 1996. He is the author of tens of thousands of poems and has published more than 3 collections.

Vivian Demuth

The Age of Extinction

A few nights ago, a bear danced around my garden carrots
and bowed to sniff the sow's scat in the soil bed.
Last summer, a deer yanked my Tibetan prayer flags
from fire-tower scaffolding
and paraded adorned antlers past trampled skulls
 in the broken forest.
I'm a human animal walking a dirt trail of illusions,
tossing vegetable scraps a mile from fire lookout
          cabin for the closest or quickest to snack.
In my first six years of alpine-solitude wrestling,
          I saw a hungry caribou outrun
          a wild six-pack of dart-gun helicopters,
heard ravens chuckle circling above loggers'
orange flagging tape alit in forest flames,
followed a scarred moose chase a fleeing Honda generator
along another new mountain road,
and took photos of a wolf pack stealing the seismic camp's
grilling steaks and biting off a page
from the First Handbook of Habitat Protection.
Over the next six years from mountain heights, I've watched
 the wildlife thin and the oil drills strike back.
Is this the Age of Extinction in which only Fortune's wheels
will roll on?

I pray that some drugged grizzly will wake up

and flip the switch.

Can a human ever gain the insight of a drugged bear?

In the meantime, I'll sit in the petrified bedrock

with what looks like a young dinosaur

and write for the unwritten record.

Vivian Demuth is the author of the eco-poetry book, Fire Watcher (Guernica Editions, 2013) and the novels, Bear War-den (Inanna Publications, 2015) and Eyes of the Forest (Smoky Peace Press,2007). Her poetry and fiction have been published in journals and anthologies in the United States, Canada, Mexico, and Europe and have been broadcast on public radio. Her website is: www.viviandemuth.com

Chris Dean

the heartland

It's been a long weekend
on the forever stretch of
I-70
taking us through Indy,
Somewhere, Illinois and
beyond.
Farms roll by
with more stops and starts
than the traffic,
fields flowing into anthill
cities
while cows graze
at the base of cellphone
towers
and drink from ponds
catching runoff from the
road.

I try to imagine what it was like
when the land fed the people
with food that fed the soul,
but it's impossible to even
try
with the ghosts of industry
blocking the view
while the passing highway
trees,
where kudzu is the only
green,

mum cautionary tales
of the shift from stewards
to pimps and strippers
that forever altered the way
the west was won.

Window down, bare feet
on the dash,
I'm not longing for some
golden, good old days
that were never all that
shiny or good.
Just sleepily watching
the blur of colors
and wondering if we missed
the last-chance exit
to build something
with sustainable worth.

I wish I was more of a dreamer.
I can't put faith in
the faithless that lack a
soul
and those I'm told are
smarter than me
haven't planned our way
out of progress
using efficiency as a North
Star.

I wiggle my toes and wonder
if I should roll up the

window
and surrender to sleep,
or if I’ve become too jaded
in my late middle-years.
Maybe it’s just hard
for me to think straight
with the haze from the
anthills and fertilizer
filling up the car.

Chris Dean, State of Indiana Beat Poet Laureate (2025-2027), writes from the heart of Indiana. Their work has been featured online, in print anthologies and they are the author of two books of poetry, Tales From a Broken Girl and We’re All Stories in the End, published by Storeylines Press.

Binod Dawadi

Birds

You fly in the sky,
Nature is your home,
You play nicely,
You sing a song,
You are in a different colours,
You call me at outside,
To enjoy with you,
You are powerful,

You tell me the life of birds,
You are full of magic,
You are lovely,
My words can't praise you,
You are our hope,
We should love birds,
You are birds,
We love you so much.

Binod Dawadi, a polymath from Kathmandu, Nepal, is a beacon of creativity, intellect, and activism. Armed with a master's degree in English, Dawadi wields the power of words to enact societal change. His journey as a writer, teacher, artist, photographer, model, and singer is a testament to his boundless passion and talent.

Paula Curci

I Was the Wilderness

- After Reading On the Road by Jack Kerouac

I was the wilderness,
the vastness,
the heart,
the soul.
The paycheck-to-paycheck.
The day to night.

Then, the ghost of the Susquehanna revealed himself
to witness life on the road.
On the Road Again.

And when I saw the muddy river,
how my heart raced.
I paced,
from boxcar to boxcar,
from town to town.
Until someone listened,
to my knowledge.
Until he heard me,
under my skirt.

I knew he separated me,
from the hobos,
from anyone I called a friend,
from the next town,
from the poetry joints.

Then the green ghost of the Susquehanna called,
to witness life on the road.
On the Road Again.

I struggled with the ghosts,
with the pot-farming pickers.
The money-making strippers.
The book-making criminals.
The wine-drinking intellectuals.

I was still learning.
I was the donut woe-man,
And I was every woe-man
struggling with the dirt
--- of the road.

Paula Curci is the Poet in Residence & Host *of Calliope's Corner: The Place Where Poets and Songwriters Meet and What's The Buzz®* at WRHU 88.7FM. She's a Poet Correspondent for *The Scene*, and a Journal to the Self® Certified Instructor. She's the Co-Founder of The Acoustic Poets Network® LLC: Poetry: It's a 'Shore' Thing® open mic, anthology, and more. Paula was the 2022-24 Poet Laureate of Nassau County, NY.

Jesse Gene Cunningham

Drums, Horns and Strings

I.

Drums beat furious
Horses' hooves
Shod with iron
Cranking gears
Turning wheels
Heart booming
Beneath animal skin
Hard stone hurling
Pelt down
Other sounds
Boulders sink below

Horns are sediment
Providing form
Stirring underwater clouds
Of mud and silt
Bray sweet harmonies
Screech brazen riffs
Fit notches and slots
Crunch out mean solid walls
Horns such heavy ballast

Strings fly elusive birds
Glimpse vague shape shadows
From the corner of the eye
Unseen when looked upon
Yet heard singing
Free from gravity

Hinting, highlighting
Dissipating wisps swell, fade
Melodies hide, bleed
Between interstices of sound
And silence

II.

The music moves
Fleeting prey
Well-oiled
Sleek, efficient
Predator machine
Breathes
Consumes
Leaves trails
Of bones
Fresh flowers
Bloom in the wake

The music falls together
As it pulls apart
Union, division
With structure, amorphous
Organic
Pulse
Expand, contract
Expand, contract
Drums
Horns
and Strings

Jesse Gene Cunningham

A longtime artist from the San Diego region, Jesse Gene Cunningham infuses his poetry with musical elements, experimenting with form and sound, always seeking to discover the mystical moment.

Curtis L. Crisler

Poemsperiment

—for Robert Glasper & his Experiment

He's mo suspicious than Elvis/
lookin over organ at fwhine
women boppin bodies to electric
shock of his insane finger play/
of his mind/ mining/
of fingers carousing down black
& white streets/ of a smokeless
new day on a YouTube joint
in Paris. It's always Paris
doing that brown-skin flight/
doing that music tight/
doing justice to just us/
hangin out in the vibery.

Robert jammin w/ songsters
now/ smellin like teen spirit/
in the black & white water
fountains/ in the amendments/
in the dogs & the niggers/
in how history helps him brew/
in the bass beggin
him back home. So/ he comes
back/ knowin not to never
forget his gots. Now/ he knows
how to capture ravens/ rocks
& rolls in hiphop recalcitrance/
how times ain't the same like

when music ate us blues &
raw.
He comes back w/ each
hand on them black & whites/
playin to a mother who
would never see a child of
hers give birth to a boy
who got the devil & god
in him/ just jazzin,
just jammin to it all/
just jazzin/
jammin/
jazzin to it
all/
just jammin/

Curtis L. Crisler was born and raised in Gary, Indiana. Crisler, an award-winning poet/author, latest book is called *Doing Drive-bys on How to Love in the Midwest.* He has six poetry books, two YA books, and five poetry chapbooks. He created the Indiana Chitlin Circuit and the poetry form called the*sonastic.* He's the Indiana Poet Laureate and Professor of English at Purdue University Fort Wayne (PFW). He can be contacted at www.poetcrisler.com.

PW Covington

Samsara

In our imperfect fermata
Of post ejaculation serenity
She whispers
“My name is Samsara.”
The trap of conditioned existence

The next accolade to be earned
The dry past for the future to drown
And erase and excuse and contextualize
Until sunrise and dusk get confused
The next acolyte to appear

Fighting for justice
The curve of your hip
Turned away from me now
On the king size
Oceanic scents fill our room

Karma wheel spinning like a jenny
Clinging to flesh in the midnights

The stigmata fermata
Strobe lights and AC Delco sparks
Set things running in the morning
A pot of coffee, percolated
A kiss upon my soul-parched lips

PW Covington writes in the Beat tradition of the North American highway. The author of numerous poetry collections, a novel, and a collection of short fiction, Covington has been named the NBPF’s New Mexico Beat Poet Laureate. When not traveling to support his writing and publishing projects, PW lives in Albuquerque’s International District, just south of Historic Route 66.

Claire Conroy

American't

No. I American't anymore.

How many families claim pride
In a relative having served
In World War Two?
Fighting Nazis in foreign lands?
Against Fascism over an ocean?
What is happening?
Right here,
Right now?
I American't anymore. In 2024.
How could escaping the will of others
Into a new land,
A place to (eventually) welcome "all".
Where freedom of self is paramount
And there's a welcome mat
In the form of a French gift, a woman.
A symbol, a beacon of acceptance.
Of, "Give Me Your Tired,
Your Poor, Your Huddled Masses
Yearning To Be Free".
Are you KIDDING me?
I American't anymore.
Where there are premiums put on the dollar
And weaknesses exploited.
I American't…
Oh! Are you a part of the spectrum?
A part of the rainbow?
Does your body restrict you

From, You?
Are you old, perhaps a vet?
Age inhibiting you from what is left?
Or does youth hold you back from
The person you feel you are?
Are you poor?
Were you born "HERE"?
English not your first language?
I American't.
Judging others and sending them blindly
To concentration camps
In a faraway place…
Shave, displaced, naked, chained.
I American't.
I certainly can not.
I can't, American't, and I will not
Agree to dumb down and live in
A world where I am not accepted
For speaking my mind,
For being my weird self,
For you being your weird self.
I will not be a part of this
Regime of persecution.
This…perversion of an idea of
"American".
Because, right now
I American't
Be proud of this flag.
Although the vows I took
As a child, to this country
Were shallow, not having full knowledge
Of the history that brought us here…

We are now here.
And I take vows taken,
In vain, as a simple child,
Seriously, while sycophants blindly
Bow and SEIG HEIL.
I American't.
AND I WON'T.

Claire Conroy, Beat Poet Laureate of Maine 2024-2026, has self published two books of poetry ("Listen" in 2018 and "Silent" in 2022) and a chapbook ("Rumors From Dead Lips" in 2024). Born in Portsmouth, NH, she is a proud board member of the Portsmouth Poet Laureate Program and is the host of their open mic, The HOOT.

Todd Cirillo

The French Quarter

Nothing compares to morning
in the French Quarter after a solid rain.
Puddles pool across the slate sidewalks
darkening them
reflecting all the colors
of Creole cottages and hurricane shutters,
yellows, greens, oranges
that burst like new suns everywhere
catching the attention of each passerby.
The leaves on the magnolias shine
as if just born,
front stoops are clean,
flags from Jazzfest wave in a tropical breeze,
the streets are clear
and the many birds
who make the Quarter home too
sing their version of Tipitina.
It all gives the feeling of a rebirth
or at the very least
an absolution of sorts.
At these times,
there's a quiet in the Quarter
that falls over everything
like glitter from a balcony.

The only movement comes
from the few clear-headed and employed
who prepare it all for the exquisite
puking and falling down chaos of later
when hand grenades and lost inhibitions reign.
By 11am, bands by the French Market
begin to beckon tourists.
Shop doors open for business.
Service industry workers get in a last smoke
before the demands of a lunch crowd,
more and more people fill the sidewalks,
courtyards, Jackson Square and the levee
with drinks in hand
to start their best day
and the Mississippi River
pays it all no mind.

Todd Cirillo was born of bastard lineage. He has many books and misdemeanors. Books include: *Sucker's Paradise, Burning the Evidence, ROXY, Three for the Road, Kisses from a Straight Razor*, and his latest, *Disposable Darlings*. His poems have appeared in numerous national and international literary journals, magazines and on cocktail napkins everywhere. Todd lives in New Orleans, Louisiana where he seeks out shiny moments and strange wisdom while looking pretty.www.toddcirillo.com

Hong Ngoc Chau

Heal The World

1

The sun always shines forever
We are happily searching ever
All the world peace for humanity
For many days in my heart truly

2

Our world is waiting for us to go far
We unite and cooperate near and far
We heal the world of me and you
A happy and rich life it will be true

3

Keep enthusiasm filled in your mind
Virtue and talent to train to love life
Care to help fellow human beings truly
Jealousy, jealousy, so we let it go truly

4

We build a good happy house, you know
Where the source of hope always grows
As full food, warm clothes, and a happy life
Harmony, kindness our friends are so fine

5

We create peace all over the world forever
Five continents and four seas are brothers

We create wealth and we reduce poverty

We deeply understand our love in reality

6

Respect the sovereignty of all countries as an option

We also help each other to progress with civilization

And fight bias we immediately erase backwardness

Pluralist cultures are always romantic more or less

7

Unanimously united with the world

Heal the world and human hearts

The faith and strength for our life

You and I are in love forever fine

Hong Ngoc Chau (Nguyen Chau Ngoc Doan Chinh)is a Master of Education Management, a member of the Ho Chi Minh City Writers Association (Vietnam) and an Honorary Doctor of Literature and Humanities of the Church and the University of Prixton. Executive member of W.U.P (World Union of Poets), General Council of the World Union of Poets with SILVER MEDAL for Researcher (14th medal of the World Union of Poets), VISHWA BHARATI Associate - India (Vishwabharati Research Center), International Ambassador of the International Council of Writers & Artists, Administrator, Coordinator, Group Expert of many literary forums around the world

Rose Cervone-Taylor

Faces of God

Faces of God
angels sent
from up above
to teach,
and connect us
to our truth.

The children
so many faces
innocent and pure
expressive,
of the love
we hold for ever
in our souls.

As we grow old
it escapes us,
till we dare to look
into their eyes.

And see the reflection
of the spark
that still lingers

in our own heart.

And we are home.

Rose Cervone-Taylor, a retired mental health professional, loves writing, photography, & travel. Rose has performed her poetry at many Nassau County venues including Molloy University. She authored several marketing booklets, & human interest stories for local Westchester & Fairfield County publications. Rose's photography & poetry exhibited at various galleries including Salmagundi Club in NYC, & other venues in the tri-state area.

Michael Ceraolo

Cleveland Haiku #674

SPEED LIMIT—-

It does not mean

Suggested Minimum Speed

Michael Ceraolo is a retired firefighter and active poet who has had three books of poetry published: Euclid Creek, from Deep Cleveland Press, and 500 Cleveland Haiku, and Lawyers, Guns, and Money from Writing Knights Press, plus numerous chapbooks.

Wendy Cartwright

Hustle

People call it a dance,
and I say they're crazy
because, if it is,
everyone I've met
has zero coordination,
no balance,
and no rhythm.

And I know that's false,
I've felt the beat,
I've been bowled over
but somehow stayed on my feet.

This is not a dance,
it is the most barbaric ritual,
performed inside an
operating theater,

while students pick apart our prowess

and criticize our skill,

hoping to learn from

the mistakes of dire consequence,

even the secondary players,

those passing the scalpel

to the back alley surgeon,

get their instruments confused

and we're left with a

hack holding a hand grenade.

Wendy Cartwright is a poet, author, photographer, and freelance journalist who lives in Columbus, Indiana. Her travels have taken her as far as Mayan Ruins and as near as the filling station. Her undiscerning tastes allow her to find creative fodder regardless of location. She has four books and has been published in various magazines, newspapers, print anthologies, and been featured in online publications. With Chris Dean, Wendy is a co-founder of Keeping the Flame Alive Press.

Patricia Carragon

Suicide

She took her own life because she had no value.

Her mother would criticize her for bad grades and sloppy penmanship,
even for not liking dolls and dresses.

Her father needed extra comfort and told her to keep it quiet . . . or else.

Her hair, body, and clothes became a schoolyard joke,
and the teacher hid behind blinders and earplugs.

Her college degree—an expensive paper paid by a bank loan—
a high price for not fitting in with company culture—
she never did get that promotion.

Her date slipped something into her drink—
she woke up in an alley with
clothes ripped, her vagina bleeding—
the blame would be hers, not his.

Her first miscarriage led to another and another,
or did the rumors of infertility make her feel less than a woman?

Her husband grew tired of her, divorced her, took the boys and house as well—
the job market, more dismal after staying home to raise the kids.

Her cancer ate her breasts and uterus—
still hungry, it spread to her intestines.

Her attempts to rebuild her life backfired, even her talents went astray—
her only accomplishment was poverty.

Her face, invisible since puberty, became her road map to nowhere,
and love couldn't find her, or did it forget her name?

Her golden years, a list of losses to outnumber her age,
but not the pills she had to take.

The list could go on—the reason was hers, not ours.

Her silent screams were real, and we never paid attention,
because suicide is a dirty word in an even dirtier world.

Who are we to judge and toss the first stone,
when she is now free and no longer in pain.

Patricia Carragon hosts Brownstone Poets and is the editor-in-chief of its annual anthology. She edits *Sense & Sensibility Haiku Journal* and is listed on the registry for *The Haiku Foundation.* Her book of jazz poetry, *Stranger on the Shore,* was accepted by Human Error Publishing for publication later this year.

Douglas G. Cala

Art's Arsenal

Watch as poets become poems,

spectate as comedians turn jokes
outside-in Listen as musicians
symphonically stir, riding riffs in
between hard-hitting lyrics, softly
delivered melodies

Call them entertainers or modern-
day troubadours Anoint them
revolutionaries, for their crafts, like
finest patchwork is woven with
meticulousness Calling us all to fore
without any forbearance

You cannot simply dismiss us

like student loans

you'd prefer not to pay,

You cannot pierce a soul in need of bearing itself
sans bravado

You cannot quell raging tides with
empty salutations, false promises,
unearned merits

We arrived at temple, in shamanic retreat

Our past livelihoods indicate we were members of
Shakespeare's

Globe Theatre We were dock workers reciting orally in-
between double shifts

We were unannounced ones, like covert messages

in bottles careening in white water waves, bottlenecking

at shorelines

Keen observations are one of our many superpowers,

Covalent bonds sharing the very best components

to serve a brighter, more urgent, now

Blades of grass that can sometimes cut into anemic skin

don't allow us to bleed out and wither

March on, speakers of mortarless
houses, Occupiers of vast
vestibules,

We may not pack stadiums just yet but

we need no artificial amplification for our

sentiments to carry globally

Get them to sign on dotted
lines, Get them to commit to
palate cleansers and mainstay,
chart-topping number ones, alike

With bold steps, prey becomes
conqueror, jungle kings,
queens copulate producing

offspring with equal wingspan

It's in fabrics, in molecules, in DNA substrates,
in vials collected from scenes of battles,
remnants of real Avengers

Watch as poets become poems,

spectate as comedians turn jokes
outside-in Listen as musicians
symphonically stir, riding riffs in

between hard-hitting lyrics,

softly delivered melodies

Douglas G. Cala is a spoken word performance poet, multimedia/IT specialist from NYC. His poetry has been published across four continents. He has performed locally, nationally and on the college circuit. He was awarded a 2025 DCLA Premier Grant from Staten Island Arts to produce "Ambrosia", a forthcoming spoken word performance poetry album.

Faruk Buzhala

Modesty Pouch

How did the actresses in hot scenes
feel
behind a modesty pouch – sweating from fatigue,
or shame, or anger from the staged friction –
I don't know, probably neither do they.
And the actors — how could they restrain the eruption
of their sleepy or alert organs
in an act of sex done and not done?

"I didn't go in — she didn't let me in,"
they say, watching the scene on screen,
then maybe they move in together
after a modesty pouch made before the cameras,
naked, rubbing, kissing, touching, clinging.

Sharon Stone, Halle Berry, Nicole Kidman,
Cameron Diaz, Penélope Cruz, and so many others
I saw in movies in some erotic scenes.
I told my friends: "It was real sex,"
they told me: "No, just acting."
I told my buddies: "It was just acting,"
they said: "No, that was real sex!"

And if we asked the actresses,
they'd probably say:
"It's just one modesty pouch —
you can't understand that."

I don't know!
But on a topic like this
if my father were asked,
he'd say:
"Hangre, s'hangre — drekë t'zihet."
(Whether you ate or not — the lunch is cooked.)

Faruk Buzhala is a Kosovar poet and writer whose work spans over three decades. His poetry captures memory, irony, and the tension between inner revolt and historical pressure. He has published several books and continues to write in both lyrical and subversive forms. His verses often blend personal and political layers through unexpected poetic twists.

John Burroughs

Bully for You

"Give to Caesar what is Caesar's and to God what is God's."

—Jesus (Mark 12:17)

President Golden Toilet and his Musky Welfare Spleen
want our attention, assets, mineral deposits, gullibility,
credibility, inability to think critically, our performative,
hypocritical so-called Christianity. They want us to buy
their inanity, feed their vanity, forget our humanity,
dispense with the Beatitudes as they demand our gratitude
and deplore our attitudes. They want to collect our "waste"
with haste, replace liberty with bigotry, justice with just "us,"
and stipulate that we capitulate to them, each God and
Caesar.

John Burroughs of Cleveland is a devoted dog dad, recent Ohio and U.S. Beat Poet Laureate, and currently serves as a vice president for the Ohio Poetry Association. His books include *Rattle and Numb* and *The Wrest of the Worthwhile*. His most recent chapbook,*Awash*, was published in July by Pure Sleeze Press. Find him at linktr.ee/johnburroughs and crisischronicles.com.

R. Bremner

You can do art

You can do art. Make the phone calls.

Latin is alone with you.

The original messenger cracked.

Everyone in town wants joy, but gets a professor.

I hear the sound of violins in a cup of black coffee.

The indifference engine estimated a monkey's time.

It is a 76% certainty that the coffee achiever has cleaned his vehicle.

The piano plays sketches of bones,

A puppet on a string drinks green beer in this town.

House cats from Elysian Fields want to spend the next year in Jerusalem.

Sea fans club a bloodrock during the night.

There is nothing left to lose for winners with no heritage.

Children sometimes wear wires on their heads.

R. Bremner A four-time honoree in the Allen Ginsberg Awards, R. Bremner has been writing of incense, peppermints, and the color of time since the 1960s, in nine books/chapbooks, and journals/anthologies including International Poetry Review, Jerry Jazz Musician, Red Wheelbarrow, Paterson Literary Review, and *Climate of Opinion: Sigmund Freud in Poetry.*Ron appeared in the legendary first issue of Passaic Review in 1979 along with Ginsberg, Laura Boss, and a plethora of sanguine young poets.

Sante "Sonny" Boninsegna, Jr.

I write my poetry for me

I write my poetry for me.
It's great if others like it
but it's my therapy.
I decide if I submit.
It's my way of processing pain.
It's my way to celebrate and commemorate the past.
It's not about financial gain
My poetry is the only thing that will last.
Good words which impact
are the pathway to immortality.
Poetry is an exclamation of joy!
An emotion and experience captured for eternity.
Writing for a special someone, about an excellent event,
Memories & our work are what we'll bequeath.
On life's road of happiness & love, poetry pays the toll.
Poetry can be celebratory or a memorial wreath.
It keeps us moving down the lonesome road,
Making our time more whole.
Etching our story on life's scroll.
Making my heart's feelings known, why someone is great,
why someone is loved!
Having it touch and enrich the subject's soul.
Delivering the message, before time is up and it's too late.
My poetry inspired out of imagination, don't need

permission.

I don't need orders or directions,

Not burdened or limited by expectation

Topic is chosen by interest

The only true task for the test

My poetry paints a scene with the language

That clearly Delivers my message.

The subject must satisfy me,

That's the key to my poetry.

I hope you enjoy it too,

but that's not what makes it true.

Peace

Sante "Sonny" Boninsegna, Jr. is a lifelong romantic and resident of the Southern Coalfields of West Virginia. Writing, WVU Sports, great food and travel are his passions. He is a graduate of Concord College ('89) and the West Virginia University College of Law ('92). He lives in Wyoming County, West Virginia.

Chris Bodor

St. Augustine Scene

Artists and musicians
on performance stages
written history leaping off the pages
the celebrated city of St. Augustine.

Neighbors and co-workers
dancing shoulder to shoulder
with tourists and far away travelers
celebrating on the same ground
where Florida tempers flared
a half a century ago
at the whites-only swimming pool
of the Monson Motor Lodge.

A melting pot fiesta
a living amends.
Festival for the eyes
so much to see.
Festival for the ears
so much to hear.
Festival for the soul
so much joy for the heart to feel.

The streets of St. Augustine

have been flooding for years

and most likely

they will be flooded for many more.

Flood of art. Flood of love. Flood of peace.

Chris Bodor is a first generation American. He was born in Connecticut to an English mother and a Hungarian father. During the past three decades, his poems have appeared in many independent, small, and micro-press publications, such as the Lummox Journal, Live Nude Poems, and New Generation Beats Anthology. He is currently serving a two-year term as the Florida State Beat Poet Laureate (2023-2025) and he is the Coordinator of the St. Augustine PoetFest.

Bengt O Björklund

time to fetter

time to fetter the phantoms and the dead
to nail their faint pulse to the floor
where no wind will dance in silence
where I will creak and break and sing
to the ghosts of living much too late

I see shadows on the move
setting sail and turning dying
into an art of blasphemy

curb the mad king dead to the sea
rein the froth and all his tales of sorrow
burning like birds or lizards or dust
before his dark pompous thrust
that only empty men can hear and heed

Bengt O Björklund, Sweden Beat Poet Laureate for life has written poetry in English for over 50 years. Soon his seventh collection will be published. Portrayed as Erich in the cult movie Midnight Express, it was there, in a Turkish jail he started to write his poetry. The Swedish group Beat Poet Society puts music to his poems. On all platforms.

Robert Bessel

Beaten

The drums boom "FREEDOM!"
The crowds stop everything
Meetings will not meet
Speeches will not be heard
Government will not ordain
Big business will not control;
It will crawl and then stop.
All of it.
Beaten.

The prophets spoke and the people heard
Lightning made everything
the way the people wanted.

Then the people saw it.
They walked it.
They fell on their knees,
not in thanks,
but because they tried the water
and nothing poured.
Because they searched for bread
and found only crumbs.
Because they shouted new words of protest

and found them gasping like fish on dry beaches.

Because they ran for their lives

knowing that no one would save them.

Because everyone was praying for the things they had beaten

Because everyone was beat

and there was nothing but freedom.

October, 2024

Robert Bessel grew up in the home town of Timothy Leary and Dr. Seuss - both inspirations for his writing. He lives in Canton, Connecticut where he recently served as First Selectman.

James Benger

The Random Trajectory of an Unfocused Lasso

The graying sky blows in yesterdays
that smell like all that could be
if we slow down the noise,
and use our unenhanced senses.

Nothing feels real these days,
but little has actually changed;
it's all real,
just as much as it ever was.

We cocoon ourselves in this oblivion,
forever looking backward,
ramming our faces right into
that lamppost we would've seen
had we only paid attention.

Sometimes I walk to
any special place of nowhere,
somewhere where nothing is,
and I feel the water trickle,
and I hear the hoot owl,
and the mud squelches
the same as it ever did.

Look under that rain-dappled leaf
browning from a winter of neglect,
you might find nothing or everything,
you might even find
why any of this has ever mattered.

We used to know,
and we still can;
it's in the atmosphere,
it hasn't left us yet.

Rope it back in,
and I'll tie it off.

James Benger is the author of several books of poetry and prose. He is on the Board of Directors of The Writers Place and the Riverfront Readings Committee, and is the founder of the 365 Poems In 365 Days online workshop, and is Editor In Chief of the anthology series. He lives in Kansas City with his wife and children.

B. Elizabeth Beck

He asks, why skeleton keys?

I don't have the answer
other than to explain, using
yet another metaphor we poets
are so fond of using when
we can't explain the inexplicable.

It's like peeling back layers
of onions, seeking the truth
to unlock mysteries even
a skeleton key can't answer

and peeling onions is stinky
work. My eyes fill with tears
stinging from stench, I cut
my finger, blood clots under
paper towel, a gift you don't
know you have until you have

a son whose blood doesn't clot.
Hemophiliac child is no joke
to a mom who wants to write
a poem that makes you laugh,
yet I'm failing since none
of this is funny except for tone
of irreverence only a survivor

can adopt yet who isn't a survivor?
The dead, I tell you. Those who
die don't survive to write a poem
intending to elicit laughs I still
won't hear from the audience

so let's return to that onion, a
yellow onion I choose from mesh
bag, testing its firmness, cutting
first, each end, then down the center
to peel back brown layers that
aren't even yellow before I dice
the way I watch chefs on videos
with knife skills I don't have. Remember?
I told you I bled but it's not so bad
I require stitches. Just a basic paper
towel, not even a band-aid because
now that my son is grown and flown
the nest, who the fuck knows
where I keep band-aids?

Task at hand, each layer
peeled enough to reach sweet
core, reward for getting that far
but I wish I could say peeling
back the layers of my childhood
only elicited a small cut on a finger
and the skeleton key is enough to
lock away memories I still have

to push away, even at my age and
let me tell you, my bones creaking
are enough evidence I'm getting old.

I wish I was mature enough to forgive
but the truth is bitterness and hatred,
contempt and anger are left in the wake
of a break-up I suffered months ago,
even though I remind myself what happened
in the past, even one day in the past is as much
the past as years ago and the onion isn't sweet
enough to staunch the blood and stop the tears
but poems are enough to write instead.

B. Elizabeth Beck is the author of five collections of poetry, including Mama Tried (Broadstone Books), winner of the American Book Fest Prize for Poetry. She is the author of the Summer Tour Trilogy. Swan Songs is her debut collection of short stories. Her work appears in journals and anthologies. Elizabeth founded two poetry series, Teen Howl and Poetry at the/ˈtā-bəl/ in Lexington, Kentucky. For more information about Elizabeth: www.elizbeck.com

Ozan Baygın (Eşref Ozan Baygın)(Eţref Ozan Baygýn)

The key record
(L.S.D)

The white lamp turned into a snail on he ceiling.

-Good point.

(He hides in his shell all the time.)

We are playing hide and seek.

(The other room at the end of the corridor is dark.)

-Run into the darkness.

-Run into the darkness.

-Run into the darkness.

That million-eyed monster is your friend.

(All alone now.)

and endless flashbacks...

Ozan Baygın (Eşref Ozan Baygın)(Eţref Ozan was born in 1993 in Istanbul (Turkey). His poems have been published in magazines and anthologies. Voice actor (Ne Nerede?)
He has published six books. In addition to this literary work, he has released seven music albums.His first English poetry book, "Forty times one thousand one" (Selected Psychedelic poems), was published by Pluton Publishing House.

Christopher Bastin

Wood and sky

Wood and sky,
wandering through pain.....
your pills concuring with my trauma
what if we revoked our beliefs,
fought with the moon
on all fours....
what if I put my foot
where my mouth once stood?
I don't know what to do with my eyes
so I shut them,
I lay down because I'm tired,
my belief system is sturdy,
I've heard many complaints, but
the back lot is jumping,
Eagles fly over California,
ravens fly over Catalina,
"Yes" plays at the Rialto and the
beavers dam the river,
I don't know what to do with my soul
so I put it aside,
I'm afraid and
I don't know if I'll make it to Spring,

the heart inside caged,

It might be my undoing!

this is the unspoken word;

Hush.......

a symphony

playing at dinner,

the truth is like the blackest cloth

to be buried in,

time sows, it's needle

darting through each hole

the recording skips

again again again

I may not be here

to fix this again,

there's only one of me

in infinite possibility, so

breathe me in

until it hurts,

I am unbuckled against

tiled moonlight,

A prostrate unlit fool

with roses

silk and somewhat

otherwise forlorn

am I safe from wisdom or

can it find me here?

there's only so much

umph and plow

beyond the tactile pins

there's no rest in restitution

no reserve in resurrection

no fin in ad infinitum

no balls in the ballet

In a pile

In a pile

lay down with me

on a mat on a pillow

on the wind

Christopher Bastin has been actively writing poetry since 2005. His interest began as a young child growing up in Oceanside, New York. He was raised in a family of art appreciation. His work will be published soon in, "The Scene", a Long Island based poetry magazine.

Dave Bartlett

Music as memoir...

The sheer take-over-your-mindedness of music, of certain songs –

grip the soul, give voice to moods, attitudes, postures…

Grade 6 (62 years ago) we lay in the park, in the dark,

behind the hedge with a transistor radio or two.

James Hold the Ladder Steady, *Me and My Cat Named Dog*,

Wolverton Mountain, *It's My Party*, *Blue Velvet*,

The Twist, *The Peppermint Twist*, *Let's Twist Again*

soon replaced by tunes of The Beatles, The Kinks, The Rolling Stones,

The Animals, then by The Byrds, Dylan -- the world opened up.

From boarding school back to my small town for Grade 11,

heading to school each day in a suede coat and wet hair

with *Like a Rolling Stone* cranked,

to make-my-mother-scream volume blaring

down the block, marching to its disaffected beat.

No wonder not a lot of teachers liked me.

Soon, find-the-song-to-match-the-mood,

or find-the-song-to-lift-the-mood.

"Wow, this acid's too heavy, put on some Donovan."

A part of personality, people judged by their taste.

"Wouldn't you love to be Gwen Stefani

when she sang I'm Just A Girl?"

Dave Bartlett has been a writer all his life while moving through a career path that included printing, proof-reading, composing room work, reporting and editing and publishing his own monthly newspaper, teaching, and finally union work. He's written non-fiction, fiction, poetry, and songs.

Carlos Barrera

Kensington

Used
to be the shelter
for these Lonestar poet's lullabies—

Traces
of forbidden passion
in the eternal darkness of her eyes.

Poisoned tongue
a thousand roadhouse stories,
cherry lips
I used to kiss at night,
when the moon
was our perpetual witness
and our shame
was guarded by the light.

Feeling like the Obvious Child,
Ulalume
was another nightmare.
I was told she had a troubled mind,
fightin'
in another warfare.

In a place
you shouldn't call back home,
filled with neon fairies,
close
to burnin' out the lights inside—
being in love
with pimp canaries.

Out of jails
built from the best intentions,
plannin' what is meant to be,
thinkin' 'bout the morning glories
and the stuff
you never dare to see.

In a vision
forged by crazy hatters,
far away from Oz & Wonderland,
the redeemers
burn their books & poetry
on the beaches of the final stand.
Singin'
for a midnight muse
with their lack of inspiration,
cryin'
for what burns inside
of a Tangiers revelation.

Written
by the drunkest poet
this old town has ever seen—
a stripper club's
kind butterfly once told me
being in love was just another sin.

In a town
that used to be like Gotham,
and the strangest of them all,
Friday nights are often lonely
when you never
hear the final call...

'Fore a missionary reaper,
who's the last hope in disguise,
you can bet
my favorite color
was the color
of her eyes—

and her lustful cherry lips,
and her skin
like alabaster,
and that purple lingerie
always
led me to disaster.

—Memories of Emilia's Room—

London's where I came to die...

Kensington has always welcomed

Lonestar poets

and lullabies.

Carlos Barrera is a writer & librarian from San Antonio, Texas. Most of his poetry is strongly influenced by folk & country music. He also wrote the novels "Freightliner" & "The Rise Of The Beast". Currently lives in Nueva Santa María, Mexico City.

Randy Barnes

Flies On Everything

Shop talk pillowed thought's mined resistance
devoured myth the haunt of who you are
love songs' gutter language thunder's heat
names in lucid meter's bitter breath
sulking gods in passionless numbers
all guesses exalted groping for hope
scars sabbath the coastlines
white souls and every faithful city
here is commitment's shaped world
vile lust and tedious appetites
soft eugenic's sea of anguish and no pearls
the deepest touch a fraudulent romanticism
the sense is don't feel but keep moving
a misshapened past in road dust and so on
free to starve any beggar's consolation
little mystery doubt bleeds through
aesthetic of terror's fed perception
keep the down in the down

and for what these sentinel shores intruding?

Randy Barnes is the Lifetime Historian/Beat Poet Laureate, Washington State, awarded in 2020. His latest book is Tactical Subterfuge: Dispatches - 2023, published by New Generation Beat Publications, 2024. He currently resides in southern Washington.

Cathy Barber

Twenty Lines

What do I have?
Twenty lines.
What can I lave
with twenty rhymes?
What else can be done
with bendy limes?
I have no mantra
I have no contra
dancing with adages
covered in bandages
This is my song
from the gut, from beyond,
from the brain
left at home in a glass.

Cathy Barber's poetry has been published across four continents and anthologized many times. She is a graduate of the Vermont College of Fine Arts MFA program and makes her home in Cleveland, Ohio, where she serves on the board of Literary Cleveland. *Once: A Golden Shovel Collection* (Kelsay Books, 2023).

Donna Allard

war musket grasses (bay of Fundy NB Canada)

I see no soldier's uniform as I walk along these shores but fresh blood cliffs, musket grasses, and a labyrinth of our relics, the unfolding of this puzzle, to figure out a broader picture, as rose-clashed with fleur de lys like an arcane coat-of-arms shared by a friend who said to follow water trails like a pirate in search of a chest, as magnet speaks closer to sand he said many have found treasures under the sheet of their own graves. Yet I favour its peaceful clay to dyed denim & origin, as I connect with those who fell for their flower & sleep in this bay of mud. Today, hooves flirt in Fundy sun, safe & watchful over my eyes, and I wonder if that story was ever passed to their off spring, since man conquers on a saddle. Come walk with me, sense the presence of their memory dancing with tides, like a final oratory along red cliffs & grassy shores. Let me retreat from time & fog. I fear ghosts & bellwalkers -

they swear the land still smells of powder.

daughter to our land

in memory of poet Rita Joe NS Canada

evening flowers close and bend

all nature is in repose.

this daughter of our land,

whose arms weigh heavy with

the many words of her people,

has penned her last reflection of life, of the world she held dear.

the Mandela flowers of hope

she held against all fear,

the raven cry that lead her forth

with the strength of Samson,

her shoulders strong as oak, and

a whisper from God this very moment brought it all to an end

it's time for your soul's gentle flight and the dragonfly

to follow, waiting to alight—

can you bare such delicate want?

Donna Allard Beat Poet Laureate

hailing from the province of New Brunswick bridges Atlantic Canada's rich poetic tradition with the legacy of the Beat movement.

Dr. Pooja Agarwal

Violence

What is violence?
Where is its seed?
Some say it's in very Nature . . .
In marshes, moors, and meads.
It is in the ferocious crashing of the waves
It is in the sudden and steamy flow of lava,
It is in the wild howling call of the beast
And in the shrieks of thunder and shots of lightning . . .

When they say this,
what they actually say
is that violence is natural
inevitable also perhaps
it is in the very order of the things,
not only in the cold sneer of the mighty kings
but also in the fervent cry of the famished soul
that yearns for nothing more than a morsel . . .!

But I say that violence is something more subtle
when a plant is watered, its eager soil absorbs
only as much as needed, and return the rest to earth,
when a tiger hunts upon a deer, it first ensures
to feed its cubs and never hoards what is superfluous

scavengers feed upon that which the tiger leaves behind
and even a dead tree is a source of food for creatures microbial . . .

Violence then is not in partaking or in satiating hunger
it is in greed that runs amok and asunder
Violence is not in the act of predation
it is in that manipulative eye called intention.
If I wish someone ill, violence would swell inside me
like waves in the sea, and should I want another's harm
violent lava will flow in my veins, only to burn me.

Like so many fine and not-so-fine ideas in the world,
Violence too has its root in human will and intention
and each time we fall prey to greed, manipulation,
or even ill intention . . . we stop being the beautiful beasts
that nature wants us to be . . . and instead, we become
quintessentially human.

Dr. Pooja Agarwal is Assistant Professor at the School of Languages, Chhatrapati Shahu Ji Maharaj University, Kanpur. She has her doctorate degree in English Literature from the Indian Institute of Technology Kanpur. Her short stories and poems have been widely published in both print and online media, including Sahitya Akademi's *Indian Literature*, and Muse India. Her first anthology of poems, *Wordless* was published by the Rhyvers Press in 2022.

Fizza Abbas

The Yellow Mirage

I have a love-hate relationship with the sun

since the moment I came into this world.

My khala tells me I'd leap at her as a child

whenever she wore her yellow dupatta during *namaz*.

I'd jump into her lap, refusing to stop

until she got too tired to hold me and handed me back to my mother.

Even then, I'd keep fussing until I was distracted by something sunny—

or a small sun on a plate: a fried egg or a half-boiled egg.

My khala would carefully prick the yolk with a silver spoon,

letting it flow —

liquid gold in a treasure hidden from the prying eyes of pirates.

I was obsessed with yellow.

I threw tantrums until my mother bought me bright yellow clothes—

nothing else. No shade lighter. No shade darker.

Even my illnesses seemed to pay homage to my love for yellow.

When I had jaundice, I remember asking my khala

why she got me a purple bracelet instead of a yellow armlet.

I even demanded a fried egg, despite the doctors forbidding it.

Reluctantly, she made one with more water than oil, calling it "pani wala anda".

When she placed it on the table, I got excited by the bubbles forming in the safaidi (albumen).

I counted them one by one,

distracted from the yolk's slightly lighter shade of yellow.

That was the first time I felt like I was swallowing the sun—

and it wasn't a good feeling. My tender mind didn't know what triggered me,

but my stomach seemed to, & it promptly rejected it

as if it had been waiting all along.

Later that night, I dreamt I was in a plane,

leaning out of the cockpit window, facing the sun, and feeling

A-L-I-V-E

The next day, I went to the rooftop, spread my arms, closed my eyes,

and let the sun's rays bathe me.

I didn't feel consumed by them,

but like I was part of the sun & those rays are my tresses—

Disheveled & uncombed.

Sunflowers became my favorite.

I'd stare at their pictures on the internet,

trying to tell them how much I adored them.

But neither did they listen, nor did I speak.

It was a tête-à-tête between silences.

At 23, I got married, but my obsession with the yellowness of the sun never waned.

At my *Mayyon*, I finally had the chance to show the world my devotion for the yellow star.

I flaunted my bright yellow sharara,

adorned with green & red stars, my body glowing with *ubtan*

& danced my heart out for the first time in front of people.

"Listen, listen, everyone, I've finally turned yellow!"

Since that day, yellow has become my symbol of happiness—

sun, my lifeline, my eclipses, my unmarked grave.

One midnight, during the early days of my marriage,

I surprised my husband by pulling out my yellow sharara and wearing it again.

Over time, I became one of those people

who feels a strange joy when someone says,

"Your eyes look yellow—are you alright?"

"Yes, I am—alive in yellow, more than they could ever know."

They'd never understand, assuming it was just one of my eccentric whims.

But in my mind, I lived in a world of yellows:

yellow desert,

yellow camels,

yellow bellies,

yellow infants.

Orange has ceased to exist for me.

Whenever I close my eyes and slip into my world of
imagined colors,

all the images I see are either black or yellow.

Once, I saw a black tunnel emitting yellow light as I entered.

I kept walking until the yellow became white,

then a blur,

and finally a dot.

Now, I'm not sure whether I truly love the sun

or simply tolerate it

because it mirrors the bright yellow world I carry within me—

a world that exists only when I close my eyes

and paint its images onto the secret notebooks

hidden in my unmarked grave.

Fizza Abbas is an independent journalist, author, and poet from Karachi, Pakistan with bylines in over 100 international poetry zines. She is also a finalist of Oxford Brookes International Poetry Competition 2021 and an author of Bakho, Ool Jalool and The Lament of the Sunken Ship. Currently, she is running an indie publishing house, BLIMPPress with her husband.

Kim Acrylic

Random Loves

He once saw God cheating on him with his wife.

Sad affairs require teenage onlookers to wear rusty toe rings to the

occasion.

His food has been fasted,

his mind is vain.

He trips through paper daisies;

the scent of wonderment amazes him.

Now just a small, bald man with a pool stick,

he passes time- awaiting his mental evaluation.

Veins tapped from his true love and ultimate

demise.

The sticky black-brown substance...

fucks him as he climaxes over and over, until he's shaking for more-always

being left for bigger, better vessels.

The whore on the corner was once his sanity-now just a mirror of

his secrets in Mexico.

Kim Acrylic, State of Washington Beat Poet Laureate (2025-2027) from Seattle, Washington, is an abstract artist and unconventional punk poet. She has been writing for over 30 years and has been featured in several anthologies. She also has two volumes of poetry available for purchase.

The National Beat Poetry Foundation, Inc.,

I founded the National Beat Poetry Foundation, Inc. to bring different perspectives to how people view the beat poets. I feel a great injustice was done in the past. My goal is to bring people together through poetry, art and music. Change the negative views and warped truths of beat poets into a positive image. I try to focus on the natural world, respect all forms of life, and help preserve what is left of the wild spaces and the Earth itself. We are all interconnected to each other. Our words matter. The beat laureates in my organization are trying to be better versions of themselves by doing good in this world. I'm building a new generation of beat poets. Freedom and growth and giving all people a voice. I did not experience that in traditional poetry circles. I wasn't accepted there. To me the word Beat means to keep evolving.

Debbie Tosun Kilday
Founder/Owner/Director
National Beat Poetry Foundation, Inc.
& It's Different Nat'l & Int'l Festivals

http://nationalbeatpoetryfoundation.org
Email - nbpf15@gmail.com

Find us on Facebook,

You Tube:
https://www.youtube.com/
@nationalbeatpoetryfoundati5845/videos

X@BeatPoetryFest)

Instagram (dtkbeatpoetnbpf)

Look for our publications:
New Generation Beat Publications
Online Magazine - BeatLife.org

www.ingramcontent.com/pod-product-compliance
Lightning Source LLC
Chambersburg PA
CBHW071235160426
43196CB00009B/1074
9781957654225